How to Use Your Mind

Title: How to Use Your Mind A Psychology of Study: Being a Manual for the Use of Students and Teachers in the Administration of Supervised Study

Author: Harry D. Kitson

Release Date: January 11, 2004 [EBook #10674]

Language: English

Character set encoding: ISO-8859-1

HOW TO USE YOUR MIND

A PSYCHOLOGY OF STUDY

BEING A MANUAL FOR THE USE OF STUDENTS AND TEACHERS IN THE ADMINISTRATION OF SUPERVISED STUDY

BY

HARRY D. KITSON, PH.D.

PROFESSOR OF PSYCHOLOGY, INDIANA UNIVERSITY

1921

PREFACE TO THE SECOND EDITION

The kindly reception accorded to the first edition of this book has confirmed the author in his conviction that such a book was needed, and has tempted him to bestow additional labor upon it. The chief changes consist in the addition of two new chapters, "Active Imagination," and "How to Develop Interest in a Subject"; the division into two parts of the unwieldy chapter on memory; the addition of readings and exercises at the end of each chapter; the preparation of an analytical table of contents; the correction of the bibliography to date; the addition of an index; and some recasting of phraseology in the interest of clearness and emphasis.

The author gratefully acknowledges the constructive suggestions of reviewers and others who have used the book, and hopes that he has profited by them in this revision.

H.D.K.

April 1, 1921.

PREFACE TO THE FIRST EDITION

Educational leaders are seeing with increasing clearness the necessity of teaching students not only the subject-matter of study but also methods of study. Teachers are beginning to see that students waste a vast amount of time and form many harmful habits because they do not know how to use their minds. The recognition of this condition is taking the form of the movement toward "supervised study," which attempts to acquaint the student with principles of economy and directness in using his mind. It is generally agreed that there are certain "tricks" which make for mental efficiency, consisting of methods of apperceiving facts, methods of review, devices for arranging work. Some are the fruits of psychological experimentation; others are derived from experience. Many of them can be imparted by instruction, and it is for the purpose of systematizing these and making them available for students that this book is prepared.

The evils of unintelligent and unsupervised study are evident to all who have any connection with modern education. They pervade the entire educational structure from kindergarten through college. In college they are especially apparent in the case of freshmen, who, in addition to the numerous difficulties incident to entrance into the college world, suffer peculiarly because they do not know how to attack the difficult subjects of the curriculum. In recognition of these conditions, special attention is given at The University of Chicago toward supervision of study. All freshmen in the School of Commerce and Administration of the University are given a course in Methods of Study, in which practical discussions and demonstrations are given regarding the ways of studying the freshman subjects. In addition to the group-work, cases presenting special features are given individual attention, for it must be admitted that while certain difficulties are common to all students, there are individual cases that present peculiar phases and these can be served only by personal consultations. These personal consultations are expensive both in time and patience, for it frequently happens that the mental habits of a student must be thoroughly reconstructed, and this requires much time and attention, but the results well repay the effort. A valuable accessory to such individual supervision over students has been found in the use of psychological tests which have been described by the author in a monograph entitled, "The Scientific Study of the College Student."[1]

[Footnote 1: Princeton University Press.]

But the college is not the most strategic point at which to administer guidance in methods of study. Such training is even more acceptably given in the high school and grades. Here habits of mental application are largely set, and it is of the utmost importance that they be set right, for the sake of the welfare of the individuals and of the institutions of higher education that receive them later. Another reason for incorporating training in methods of study into secondary and elementary schools is that more individuals will be helped, inasmuch as the eliminative process has not yet reached its culmination.

In high schools where systematic supervision of study is a feature, classes are usually conducted in Methods of Study, and it is hoped that this book will meet the demand for a text-book for such classes, the material being well within the reach of high school students. In high schools where instruction in Methods of Study is given as part of a course in elementary psychology, the book should also prove useful, inasmuch as it gives a summary of psychological principles relating to the cognitive processes.

In the grades the book cannot be put into the hands of the pupils, but it should be mastered by the teacher and applied in her supervising and teaching activities. Embodying, as it does, the results of researches in educational psychology, it should prove especially suitable for use in teachers' reading circles where a concise presentation of the facts regarding the psychology of the learning process is desired.

There is another group of students who need training in methods of study. Brain workers in business and industry feel deeply the need of greater mental efficiency and seek eagerly for means to attain it. Their earnestness in this search is evidenced by the success of various systems for the training of memory, will, and other mental traits. Further evidence is found in the efforts of many corporations to maintain schools and classes for the intellectual improvement of their employees. To all such the author offers the work with the hope that it may be useful in directing them toward greater mental efficiency.

In courses in Methods of Study in which the book is used as a class-text, the instructor should lay emphasis not upon memorization of the facts in the book, but upon the application of them in study. He should expect to see parallel with progress through the book, improvement in the mental ability of the students. Specific problems may well be arranged on the basis of the subjects of the curriculum, and students should be urged to utilize the suggestions immediately. The subjects treated in the book are those which the author has found in his experience with college students to constitute the most frequent sources of difficulty, and under these conditions, the sequence of topics followed in the book has seemed most favorable for presentation. With other groups of students, however, another sequence of topics may be found desirable; if so, the order of topics may be changed. For example, in case the chapter on brain action is found to presuppose more physiological knowledge than that possessed by the students, it may be omitted or may be used merely for reference when enlightenment is desired upon some of the physiological descriptions in later chapters. Likewise, the chapter dealing with intellectual difficulties of college students may be omitted with non-collegiate groups.

The heavy obligation of the author to a number of writers will be apparent to one familiar with the literature of theoretical and educational psychology. No attempt is made to render specific acknowledgments, but special mention should be made of the large draughts made upon the two books by Professor Stiles which treat so helpfully of the bodily relations of the student. These books contain so much good sense and scientific information that they should receive a prominent place among the books recommended to students. Thanks are due to Professor Edgar James Swift and Charles Scribner's Sons for permission to use a figure from "Mind in the Making"; and to J.B. Lippincott Company for adaptation of cuts from Villiger's "Brain and Spinal Cord."

The author gratefully acknowledges helpful suggestions from Professors James R. Angell, Charles H. Judd and C. Judson Herrick, who have read the greater part of the manuscript and have commented upon it to its betterment. The obligation refers, however, not only to the immediate preparation of this work but also to the encouragement which, for several years, the author has received from these scientists, first as student, later as colleague.

THE AUTHOR.

CHICAGO, September 25, 1916.

CONTENTS

CHAPTER

I.

INTELLECTUAL PROBLEMS OF THE COLLEGE FRESHMAN

Number. Variety. Lecture Method. Note Taking. Amount of Library Work. High Quality Demanded. Necessity for Making Schedule. A College Course Consists in the Formation of Habits. Requires Active Effort on Part of Student. Importance of Good Form.

II. NOTE TAKING

Uses of Notes. LECTURE NOTES--Avoid Verbatim Reports. Maintain Attitude of Mental Activity. Seek Outline Chiefly. Use Notes in Preparing Next Lesson. READING NOTES--Summarize Rather Than Copy. Read With Questions in Mind. How to Read. How to Make Bibliographies. LABORATORY NOTES--Content. Form. Miscellaneous Hints.

III. BRAIN ACTION DURING STUDY

The Organ of Mind. Gross Structure. Microscopic Structure. The Neurone. The Nervous Impulse. The Synapse. Properties of Nervous Tissue --Impressibility, Conductivity, Modifiability. Pathways Used in

Study--Sensory, Motor, Association. Study is a Process of Making Pathways in Brain.

IV. FORMATION OF STUDY-HABITS

Definition of Habit. Examples. Inevitableness of Habits in Brain and Nervous System. How to Insure Useful Habits--Choose What Shall Enter; Choose Mode of Entrance; Choose Mode of Egress; Go Slowly at First; Observe Four Maxims. Advantages and Disadvantages of Habit. Ethical Consequences.

V. ACTIVE IMAGINATION

Nature of the Image. Its Use in Imagination. Necessity for Number, Variety, Sharpness. Source of "Imaginative" Productions. Method of Developing Active Imaginative Powers: Cultivate Images in Great Number, Variety, Sharpness; Actively Combine the Elements of Past Experience.

VI. FIRST AIDS TO MEMORY--IMPRESSION

Four Phases. Conditions of Impression: Care, Clearness, Choice of Favorable Sense Avenue, Repetition, Overlearning, Primacy, Distribution of Repetitions, (Inferences Bearing Upon Theme-writing), "Whole" vs. "Part" Method, "Rote" vs. "logical" Method, Intention.

VII. SECOND AIDS TO MEMORY--RETENTION, RECALL AND RECOGNITION

Retention. Recall. Recall Contrasted With Impression. Practise Recall in Impression. Recognition. Advantages of Review. Memory Works According to Law. Possibility of Improvement. Connection With Other Mental Processes.

VIII. CONCENTRATION OF ATTENTION

Importance in Mental Life. Analysis of Concrete Attentive State. Cross-section of Mental Stream. Focal Object, Clear; Marginal Objects, Dim. Fluctuation. Ease of Concentration Requires (1) Removal of All

Marginal Distractions Possible, (2) Ignoring Others. Conditions Favorable for Concentration. Relation to Other Mental Processes.

IX. HOW WE REASON

Reasoning Contrasted with Simpler Mental Operations. Illustrated by Method of Studying Geometry. Analysis of Reasoning Act: Recognition of Problem, Efforts to Solve It, Solution. Study in Problems. Requirements for Effective Reasoning: Many Ideas, Accessible, Clear. How to Clarify Ideas: Define, Classify. Relation Between Habit and Reasoning. Summary.

X. EXPRESSION AS AN AID IN STUDY

Expression an Inevitable Accompaniment of Nervous Activity. Extent of Expressive Movements. Relation Between Ideas and Expressive Acts. Ethical Considerations. Methods of Expression Chiefly Used in Study: Speech, Writing, Drawing. Effects of Expression: (1) On Brain, (2) On Ideas. Hints on Development of Freedom of Expression.

XI. HOW TO BECOME INTERESTED IN A SUBJECT

Nature of Interest. Intellectual Interests Gained Through Experience. Many Possible Fields of Interest. Laws of Interest.

XII. THE PLATEAU OF DESPOND

Measurement of Mental Progress. Analysis of the "Learning Curve." Irregularity. Rapid Progress at Beginning. The Plateau. Causes. Remedies.

XIII. MENTAL SECOND-WIND

Description: (1) Physical, (2) Mental. Hidden Sources of Energy. Retarding Effect of Fatigue. Analysis of Fatigue. How to Reduce Fatigue in Study.

XIV. EXAMINATIONS

HOW TO USE YOUR MIND

CHAPTER I

INTELLECTUAL PROBLEMS OF THE COLLEGE FRESHMAN

In entering upon a college course you are taking a step that may completely revolutionize your life. You are facing new situations vastly different from any you have previously met. They are also of great variety, such as finding a place to eat and sleep, regulating your own finances, inaugurating a new social life, forming new friendships, and developing in body and mind. The problems connected with mental development will engage your chief attention. You are now going to use your mind more actively than ever before and should survey some of the intellectual difficulties before plunging into the fight.

Perhaps the first difficulty you will encounter is the substitution of the lecture for the class recitation to which you were accustomed in high school. This substitution requires that you develop a new technic of learning, for the mental processes involved in an oral recitation are different from those used in listening to a lecture. The lecture system implies that the lecturer has a fund of knowledge about a certain field and has organized this knowledge in a form that is not duplicated in the literature of the subject. The manner of presentation, then, is unique and is the only means of securing the knowledge in just that form. As soon as the words have left the mouth of the lecturer they cease to be accessible to you. Such conditions require a unique mental attitude and unique mental habits. You will be obliged, in the first place, to maintain sustained attention over long periods of time. The situation is not like that in reading, in which a temporary lapse of attention may be remedied by turning back and rereading. In listening to a lecture, you are obliged to catch the words "on the fly." Accordingly you must develop new habits of paying attention. You will also need to develop a new technic for memorizing, especially for memorizing things heard. As a partial aid in this, and also for purposes of organizing material received in lectures, you will need to develop ability to take notes. This is a process with which you have heretofore had little to do. It is a most important phase of college life, however, and will repay earnest study.

Another characteristic of college study is the vast amount of reading required. Instead of using a single text-book for each course, you may use several. They may cover great historical periods and represent the ideas of many men. In view of the amount of reading assigned, you will also be obliged to learn to read faster. No longer will you have time to dawdle sleepily through the pages of easy texts; you will have to cover perhaps fifty or a hundred pages of knotty reading every day. Accordingly you must learn to handle books expeditiously and to comprehend quickly. In fact, economy must be your watchword throughout. A German lesson in high school may cover thirty or forty lines a day, requiring an hour's preparation. A German assignment in college, however, may cover four or five or a dozen pages, requiring hard work for two or three hours.

You should be warned also that college demands not only a greater quantity but also a higher quality of work. When you were a high school student the world expected only a high school student's accomplishments of you. Now you are a college student, however, and your intellectual responsibilities have increased. The world regards you now as a person of considerable scholastic attainment and expects more of you than before. In academic terms this means that in order to attain a grade of 95 in college you will have to work much harder than you did for that grade in high school, for here you have not only more difficult subject-matter, but also keener competition for the first place. In high school you may have been the brightest student in your class. In college, however, you encounter the brightest students from many schools. If your merits are going to stand out prominently, therefore, you must work much harder. Your work from now on must be of better quality.

Not the least of the perplexities of your life as a college student will arise from the fact that no daily schedule is arranged for you. The only time definitely assigned for your work is the fifteen hours a week, more or less, spent in the class-room. The rest of your schedule must be arranged by yourself. This is a real task and will require care and thought if your work is to be done with greatest economy of time and effort.

This brief survey completes the catalogue of problems of mental development that will vex you most in adjusting your methods of study to college conditions. In order to make this adjustment you will be obliged to form a number of new habits. Indeed, as you become more and more expert as a student, you will see that the whole process resolves itself into one of habit-formation, for while a college education has two phases--the acquisition of facts and the formation of habits--it is the latter which is the more important. Many of the facts that you learn will be forgotten; many will be outlawed by time; but the habits of study you form will be permanent possessions. They will consist of such things as methods of grasping facts, methods of reasoning about facts, and of concentrating attention. In acquiring these habits you must have some material upon which you may concentrate your attention, and it will be supplied by the subjects of the curriculum. You will be asked, for instance, to write innumerable themes in courses in English composition; not for the purpose of enriching the world's literature, nor for the delectation of your English instructor, but for the sake of helping you to form habits of forceful expression. You will be asked to enter the laboratory and perform numerous experiments, not to discover hitherto unknown facts, but to obtain practice in scientific procedure and to learn how to seek knowledge by yourself. The curriculum and the faculty are the means, but you yourself are the agent in the educational process. No matter how good the curriculum or how renowned the faculty, you cannot be educated without the most vigorous efforts on your part. Banish the thought that you are here to have knowledge "pumped into" you. To acquire an education you must establish and maintain not a passive attitude but an active attitude. When you go to the gymnasium to build up a good physique, the physical director does not tell you to hold yourself limp and passive while he pumps your arms and legs up and down. Rather he urges you to put forth effort, to exert yourself until you are tired. Only by so doing can you develop physical power. This principle holds true of mental development. Learning is not a process of passive "soaking-in." It is a matter of vigorous effort, and the harder you work the more powerful you become. In securing a college education you are your own master.

In the development of physical prowess you are well aware of the importance of doing everything in "good form." In such sports as swimming and hurdling, speed and grace depend primarily upon it. The same principle holds true in the development of the mind. The most serviceable mind is that which accomplishes results in the shortest time and with least waste motion. Take every precaution, therefore, to rid yourself of all superfluous and impeding methods.

Strive for the development of good form in study. Especially is this necessary at the start. Now is the time when you are laying the foundations for your mental achievements in college. Keep a sharp lookout, then, at every point, to see that you build into the foundation only those materials and that workmanship which will support a masterly structure.

READINGS AND EXERCISES

NOTE.--Numbers in parentheses refer to complete citations in Bibliography at end of book.

Readings: Fulton (5) Lockwood (11)

Exercise 1. List concrete problems that have newly come to you since your arrival upon the campus.

Exercise 2. List in order the difficulties that confront you in preparing your daily lessons.

Exercise 3. Prepare a work schedule similar to that provided by the form in Chart I. Specify the subject with which you will be occupied at each period.

Exercise 4. Try to devise some way of registering the effectiveness with which you carry out your schedule. Suggestions are contained in the summary: Disposition of (1) as planned; (2) as spent. To divide the number of hours wasted by 24 will give a partial "index of efficiency."

CHAPTER II

NOTE-TAKING

Most educated people find occasion, at some time or other, to take notes. Although this is especially true of college students, they have little success, as any college instructor will testify. Students, as a rule, do not realize that there is any skill involved in taking notes. Not until examination time arrives and they try vainly to labor through a maze of scribbling, do they realize that there must be some system in note-taking. A careful examination of note-taking shows that there are rules or principles, which, when followed, have much to do with increasing ability in study.

One criterion that should guide in the preparation of notes is the use to which they will be put. If this is kept in mind, many blunders will be saved. Notes may be used in three ways: as material for directing each day's study, for cramming, and for permanent, professional use. Thus a note-book may be a thing of far-reaching value. Notes you take now as a student may be valuable years hence in professional life. Recognition of this will help you in the preparation of your notes and will determine many times how they should be prepared.

The chief situations in college which require note-taking are lectures, library reading and laboratory work. Accordingly the subject will be considered under these three heads.

LECTURE NOTES.--When taking notes on a lecture, there are two extremes that present themselves, to take exceedingly full notes or to take almost no notes. One can err in either direction. True, on first thought, entire stenographic reports of lectures appear desirable, but second thought will show that they may be dispensed with, not only without loss, but with much gain. The most obvious objection is that too much time would be consumed in transcribing short-hand notes. Another is that much of the material in a lecture is undesirable for permanent possession. The instructor repeats much for the sake of emphasis; he multiplies illustrations, not important in themselves, but important for the sake of stressing his point. You do not need these illustrations in written form, however, for once the point is made you rarely need to depend upon the illustrations for its retention. A still more cogent objection is that if you occupy your attention with the task of copying the lecture verbatim, you do not have time to think, but become merely an automatic recording machine. Experienced stenographers say that they form the habit of recording so automatically that they fail utterly to comprehend the meaning of what is said. You as a student cannot afford to have your attention so distracted from the meaning of the lecture, therefore reduce your classroom writing to a minimum.

Probably the chief reason why students are so eager to secure full lecture notes is that they fear to trust their memory. Such fears should be put at rest, for your mind will retain facts if you pay close attention and make logical associations during the time of impression. Keep your mind free, then, to work upon the subject-matter of the lecture. Debate mentally with the speaker. Question his statements, comparing them with your own experience or with the results of your study. Ask yourself frequently, "Is that true?" The essential thing is to maintain an attitude of mental activity, and to avoid anything that will reduce this and make you passive. Do not think of yourself as a vat into which the instructor pumps knowledge. Regard yourself rather as an active force, quick to perceive and to comprehend meaning, deliberate in acceptance and firm in retention.

After observing the stress laid, throughout this book, upon the necessity for logical associations, you will readily see that the key-note to note-taking is, Let your notes represent the logical progression of thought in the lecture. Strive above all else to secure the skeleton--the framework upon which the lecture is hung. A lecture is a logical structure, and the form in which it is presented is the outline. This outline, then, is your chief concern. In the case of some lectures it is an easy matter. The lecturer may place the outline in your hands beforehand, may present it on the black-board, or may give it orally. Some lecturers, too, present their material in such clear-cut divisions that the outline is easily followed. Others, however, are very difficult to follow in this regard.

In arranging an outline you will find it wise to adopt some device by which the parts will stand out prominently, and the progression of thought will be indicated with proper subordination of titles. Adopt some system at the beginning of your college course, and use it in all your notes. The system here given may serve as a model, using first the Roman numerals, then capitals, then Arabic numerals:

I. II. A. B. 1. 2. a. b. (1) (2) (a) (b)

In concluding this discussion of lecture notes, you should be urged to make good use of your notes after they are taken. First, glance over them as soon as possible after the lecture. Inasmuch as they will then be fresh in your mind, you will be able to recall almost the entire lecture; you will also be able to supply missing parts from memory. Some students make it a rule to reduce all class-notes to typewritten form soon after the lecture. This is an excellent practice, but is rather expensive in time. In addition to this after-class review, you should make a second review of your notes as the first step in the preparation of the next day's lesson. This will connect up the lessons with each other and will make the course a unified whole instead of a series of disconnected parts. Too often a course exists in a student's mind as a series of separate discussions and he sees only the horizon of a single day. This condition might be represented by a series of disconnected links:

O O O O O

A summary of each day's lesson, however, preceding the preparation for the next day, forges new links and welds them all together into an unbroken chain:

OOOOOOOOOO

A method that has been found helpful is to use a double-page system of notetaking, using the left-hand page for the bare outline, with largest divisions, and the right-hand page for the details. This device makes the note-book readily available for hasty review or for more extended study.

READING NOTES.--The question of full or scanty notes arises in reading notes as in lecture notes. In general, your notes should represent a summary, in your own words, of the author's discussion, not a duplication of it. Students sometimes acquire the habit of reading single sentences at a time, then of writing them down, thinking that by making an exact copy of the book, they are playing safe. This is a pernicious practice; it spoils continuity of thought and application. Furthermore, isolated sentences mean little, and fail grossly to represent the real thought of the author. A better way is to read through an entire paragraph or section, then close the book and reproduce in your own words what you have read. Next, take your summary and compare with the original text to see that you have really grasped the point. This procedure will be beneficial in several ways. It will encourage continuous concentration of attention to an entire argument; it will help you to preserve relative emphasis of parts; it will lead you to regard thought and not words. (You are undoubtedly familiar with the state of mind wherein you find yourself reading merely words and not following the thought.) Lastly, material studied in this way is remembered longer than material read scrappily. In short, such a method of reading makes not only for good memory, but for good mental habits of all kinds. In all your reading, hold to the conception of yourself as a thinker, not a sponge. Remember, you do not need to accept unqualifiedly everything you read. A worthy ideal for every student to follow is expressed in the motto carved on the wall of the great reading-room of the Harper Memorial Library at The University of Chicago: "Read not to contradict, nor to believe, but to weigh and consider." Ibsen bluntly states the same thought:

"Don't read to swallow; read to choose, for 'Tis but to see what one has use for."

Ask yourself, when beginning a printed discussion, What am I looking for? What is the author going to talk about? Often this will be indicated in topical headings. Keep it in the background of your mind while reading, and search for the answer. Then, when you have read the necessary portion, close the book and summarize, to see if the author furnished what you sought. In short, always read for a purpose. Formulate problems and seek their solutions. In this way will there be direction in your reading and your thought.

This discussion of reading notes has turned into an essay on "How to Read," and you must be convinced by this time that there is much to learn in this respect, so much that we may profitably spend more time in discussing it.

Every book you take up should be opened with some preliminary ceremony. This does not refer to the physical operation of opening a new book, but to the mental operation. In general, take the following steps:

1. Observe the title. See exactly what field the book attempts to cover.

2. Observe the author's name. If you are to use his book frequently, discover his position in the field. Remember, you are going to accept him as authority, and you should know his status. You may be told this on the title-page, or you may have to consult Who's Who, or the biographical dictionary.

3. Glance over the preface. Under some circumstances you should read it carefully. If you are going to refer to the book very often, make friends with the author; let him introduce himself to you; this he will do in the preface. Observe the date of publication, also, in order to get an idea as to the recency of the material.

4. Glance over the table of contents. If you are very familiar with the field, and the table of contents is outlined in detail, you might advantageously study it and dispense with reading the book. On the

other hand, if you are going to consult the book only briefly, you might find it necessary to study the table of contents in order to see the relation of the part you read to the entire work.

5. Use the index intelligently; it may save you much time.

You will have much to do throughout your college course with the making of bibliographies, that is, with the compilation of lists of books bearing upon special topics. You may have bibliographies given you in some of your courses, or you may be asked to compile your own. Under all circumstances, prepare them with the greatest care. Be scrupulous in giving references. There is a standard form for referring to books and periodicals, as follows:

C.R. Henderson, Industrial Insurance (2d ed.; Chicago: The University of Chicago Press, 1912), p. 321.

S.I. Curtis, "The Place of Sacrifice," Biblical World, Vol. XXI (1902), p. 248 *ff.*

LABORATORY NOTES.--The form for laboratory notes varies with the science and is usually prescribed by the instructor. Reports of experiments are usually written up in the order: Object, Apparatus, Method, Results, Conclusions. When detailed instructions are given by the instructor, follow them accurately. Pay special attention to neatness. Instructors say that the greatest fault with laboratory note-books is lack of neatness. This reacts upon the instructor, causing him much trouble in correcting the note-book. The resulting annoyance frequently prejudices him, against his will, against the student. It is safe to assert that you will materially increase your chances of a good grade in a laboratory course by the preparation of a neat note-book.

The key-note of the twentieth century is economy, the tendency in all lines being toward the elimination of waste. College students should adopt this aim in the regulation of their study affairs, and there is much opportunity for applying it in note-taking. So far, the discussion has had to do with the *content* of the note-book, but *its form* is equally important. Much may be done by utilization of mechanical devices to save time and energy.

First, write in ink. Pencil marks blur badly and become illegible in a few months. Remember, you may be using the notebook twenty years hence, therefore make it durable.

Second, write plainly. This injunction ought to be superfluous, for common sense tells us that writing which is illegible cannot be read even by the writer, once it has "grown cold." Third, take care in forming sentences. Do not make your notes consist simply of separate, scrappy jottings. True, it is difficult, under stress, to form complete sentences. The great temptation is to jot down a word here and there and trust to luck or an indulgent memory to supply the context at some later time. A little experience, however, will quickly demonstrate the futility of such hopes; therefore strive to form sensible phrases, and to make the parts of the outline cohere. Apply the principles of English composition to the preparation of your note-book.

A fourth question concerns size and shape of the note-book. These features depend partly upon the nature of the course and partly upon individual taste. It is often convenient and practicable to keep the notes for all courses in a single note-book. Men find it advantageous to use a small note-book of a size that can be carried in the coat pocket and studied at odd moments.

A fifth question of a mechanical nature is, Which is preferable, bound or loose-leaf note-books? Generally the latter will be found more desirable. Leaves are easily inserted and the sections are easily filed on completion of a course.

It goes without saying that the manner in which notes, are to be taken will be determined by many factors, such as the nature of individual courses, the wishes of instructors, personal tastes and habits. Nevertheless, there are certain principles and practices which are adaptable to nearly all conditions, and it is these that we have discussed. Remember, note-taking is one of the habits you are to form in college. See that the habit is started rightly. Adopt a good plan at the start and adhere to it. You may be encouraged, too, with the thought that facility in note-taking will come with practice. Note-taking is an art and as you practise you will develop skill.

We have noted some of the most obvious and immediate benefits derived from well-prepared notes, consisting of economy of time, ease of review, ease of permanent retention. There are other benefits, however, which, though less obvious, are of far greater importance. These are the permanent effects upon the mind. Habits of correct thinking are the chief result of correct note-taking. As you develop in this particular ability, you will find corresponding improvement in your ability to comprehend and assimilate ideas, to retain and reproduce facts, and to reason with thoroughness and independence.

READINGS AND EXERCISES

Readings:

Adams (1) Chapter VIII.

Dearborn (2) Chapter II.

Kerfoot (10)

Seward (17)

Exercise 1. Contrast the taking of notes from reading and from lectures.

Exercise 2. Make an outline of this chapter.

Exercise 3. Make an outline of some lecture.

CHAPTER III

BRAIN ACTION DURING STUDY

Though most people understand more or less vaguely that the brain acts in some way during study, exact knowledge of the nature of this action is not general. As you will be greatly assisted in understanding mental processes by such knowledge, we shall briefly examine the brain and its connections. It will be manifestly impossible to inquire into its nature very minutely, but by means of a description you will be able to secure some conception of it and thus will be able better to control the mental processes which it underlies.

To the naked eye the brain is a large jelly-like mass enclosed in a bony covering, about one-fourth of an inch thick, called the skull. Inside the skull it is protected by a thick membrane. At its base emerges the spinal cord, a long strand of nerve fibers extending down the spine. For most of its length, the cord is about as large around as your little finger, but it tapers at the lower end. From it at right angles throughout its length branch out thirty-one pairs of fibrous nerves which radiate to all parts of the body. The brain and spinal cord, with all its ramifications, are known as the nervous system. You see now that, though we started with the statement that the mind is intimately connected with the brain, we must now enlarge our statement and say it is connected with the entire nervous system. It is therefore to the nervous system that we must turn our attention.

Although to the naked eye the nervous system is apparently made up of a number of different kinds of material, still we see, when we turn our microscopes upon it, that its parts are structurally the same. Reduced to lowest terms, the nervous system is found to be composed of minute units of structure called nerve-cells or neurones. Each of these looks like a string frayed out at both ends, with a bulge somewhere along its length. The nervous system is made up of millions of these little cells packed together in various combinations and distributed throughout the body. Some of the neurones are as long as three feet; others measure but a fraction of an inch in length.

We do not know exactly how the mind, that part of us which feels, reasons and wills, is connected with this mass of cells called the nervous system. We do know, however, that every time anything occurs in the mind, there is a change in some part of the nervous system. Applying this fact to study, it is obvious that when you are performing any of the operations of study, memorizing foreign vocabularies, making arithmetical calculations, reasoning out problems in geometry, you are making changes in your nervous system. The question before us, then, is, What is the nature of these changes?

According to present knowledge, the action of the nervous system is best conceived as a form of chemical change that spreads among the nerve-cells. We call this commotion the nervous current. It is very rapid, moving faster than one hundred feet a second, and runs along the cells in much the same way as a "spark runs along a train of gunpowder." It is important to note that neurones never act singly; they always act in groups, the nervous current passing from neurone to neurone. It is thought that the most important changes in the nervous system do not occur within the individual neurones, but at the points where they join with each other. This point of connection is called the synapse and although we do not understand its exact nature, it may well be pictured as a valve that governs the passage of the nervous current from neurone to neurone. At time of birth, most of the valves are closed. Only a few are open, mainly those connected with the vegetative processes such as breathing and digestion. But as the individual is played upon by the objects of the environment, the valves open to the passage of the nervous current. With increased use they become more and more permeable, and thus learning is the process of making easier the passage of the nervous current from one neurone to another.

We shall secure further light upon the action of the nervous system if we examine some of the properties belonging to nerve-cells. The first one is *impressibility*. Nerve-cells are very sensitive to impressions from the outside. If you have ever had the dentist touch an exposed nerve, you know how extreme this sensitivity is. Naturally such a property is very important in education, for had we not the power to receive impressions from the outside world we should not be able to acquire knowledge. We should not even be able to perceive danger and remove ourselves from harm. "If we compare a man's body to a building, calling the steel frame-work his skeleton and the furnace and power station his digestive organs and lungs, the nervous system would include, with other things, the thermometers, heat regulators, electric buttons, door-bells, valve-openers,--the parts of the building, in short, which are specifically designed to respond to influences of the environment." The second property of nerve-cells which is important in study is *conductivity*. As soon as a neurone is stimulated at one end, it communicates its excitement, by means of the nervous current, to the next neurone or to neighboring neurones. Just as an electric current might pass along one wire, thence to another, and along it to a third, so the nervous current passes from neurone to neurone. As might be expected, the two functions of impressibility and conductivity are aided by such an arrangement of the nerve-cells that the nervous current may pass over definitely laid pathways. These systems of pathways will be described in a later paragraph.

The third property of nerve-cells which is important in study is *modifiability*. That is, impressions made upon the nerve-cells are retained. Most living tissue is modifiable to some extent. The features of the face are modifiable, and if one habitually assumes a peevish expression, it becomes, after a time, permanently fixed. The nervous system, however, possesses the power of modifiability to a marked degree, even a single impression sufficing to make striking modification. This is very important in study, being the basis for the retentive powers of the mind.

Having examined the action of the nervous system in its simplicity, we have now to examine the ways in which the parts of the nervous system are combined. We shall be helped if we keep to the conception of it as an aggregation of systems or groups of pathways. Some of these we shall attempt to trace out. Beginning with those at the outermost parts of the body, we find them located in the sense-organs, not only within the traditional five, but also within the muscles, tendons, joints, and internal organs of the body such as the heart, and digestive organs. In all these places we find ends of neurones which converge at the spinal cord and travel to the brain. They are called sensory neurones and their function is to carry messages inward to the brain. Thus, the brain represents, in great part, a central receiving station for impressions from the outside world. The nerve-cells carrying messages from the various parts of the body terminate in particular areas. Thus an area in the back part of the brain receives messages from the eyes; another area near the top of the brain receives messages from the skin. These areas are quite clearly marked out and may be studied in detail by means of the accompanying diagram.

There is another large group of nerve-cells which, when traced out, are found to have one terminal in the brain and the other in the muscles throughout the body. The area in the brain, where these neurones emerge, is near the top of the brain in the area marked *Motor* on the diagram. From here the fibers travel down through the spinal cord and out to the muscles. The nerve-cells in this group are called motor neurones and their function is to carry messages from the brain out to the muscles, for a muscle ordinarily does not act without a nervous current to set it off.

So far we have seen that the brain has the two functions of receiving impressions from the sense-organs and of sending out orders to the muscles. There is a further mechanism that must now be described. When messages are received in the sensory areas, it is necessary that there be some means within the brain of transmitting them over to the motor area so that they may be acted upon. Such an arrangement is provided by another group of nerve-cells in the brain, having as their function the transmission of the nervous current from one area to another. They are called association neurones and transmit the nervous current from sensory areas to motor areas or from one sensory area to another. For example, suppose you see a brick falling from above and you dodge quickly back. The neural action accompanying this occurrence consists of an impression upon the nerve-cells in the eye, the conduction of the nervous current back to the visual area of the brain, the transmission of the current over association neurones to the motor area, then its transmission over the motor neurones, down the spinal cord, to the muscles that enable you to dodge the missile. The association neurones have the further function of connecting one sensory area in the brain with another. For example, when you see, smell, taste and touch an orange, the corresponding areas in the brain act in conjunction and are associated by means of the association neurones connecting them. The association neurones play a large part in the securing and organizing of knowledge. They are very important in study, for all learning consists in building up associations.

From the foregoing description we see that the nervous system consists merely of a mechanism for the reception and transmission of incoming messages and their transformation into outgoing messages which produce movement. The brain is the center where such transformations are made, being a sort of central switchboard which permits the sense-organs to come into communication with muscles. It is also the instrument by means of which the impressions from the various senses can be united and experience can be unified. The brain serves further as the medium whereby impressions once made can be retained. That is, it is the great organ of memory. Hence we see that it is to this organ we must look for the performance of the activities necessary to study. Everything that enters it produces some modification within it. Education consists in a process of undergoing a selected group of experiences of such a nature as to leave beneficial results in the brain. By means of the changes made there, the individual is able better to adjust himself to new situations. For when the individual enters the world, he is not prepared to meet many situations; only a few of the neural connections are made and he is able to perform only a meagre number of simple acts, such as breathing, crying, digestion. The pathways for complex acts, such as speaking English or French, or writing, are not formed at birth but must be built up within the life-time of the individual. It is the process of building them up that we call education. This process is a physical feat involving the production of changes in physical material in the brain. Study involves the overcoming of resistance in the nervous system. That is why it is so hard. In your early school-days, when you set about laboriously learning the multiplication table, your unwilling protests were wrung because you were being compelled to force the nervous current through new pathways, and to overcome the inertia of physical matter. Today, when you begin a train of reasoning, the task is difficult because you are opening hitherto untravelled pathways. There is a comforting thought, however, which is derived from the factor of modifiability, in that with each succeeding repetition, the task becomes easier, because the path becomes worn smoothly and the nervous current seeks it of its own accord; in other words, each act and each thought tends to become habitualized. Education is then a process of forming habits, and the rest of the book will be devoted to the description and discussion of habits which a student should form.

READING AND EXERCISE

Reading: Herrick (7)

Exercise 1. Draw a picture of the brain, showing roughly what takes place there (a) when you read a book, (6) listen to a lecture, (c) take notes.

CHAPTER IV

FORMATION OF STUDY-HABITS

As already intimated, this book adopts the view that education is a process of forming habits in the brain. In the formation of habits there are several principles that must be observed. Accordingly we shall devote a chapter to the consideration of habits in general before discussing the specific habits involved in various kinds of study.

Habit may be defined roughly as the tendency to act time after time in the same way. Thus defined, you see that the force of habit extends throughout the entire universe. It is a habit for the earth to revolve on its axis once every twenty-four hours and to encircle the sun once every year. When a pencil falls from your hand it has a habit of dropping to the floor. A piece of paper once folded tends to crease in the same place. These are examples of the force of habit in nonliving matter. Living matter shows its power even more clearly. If you assume a petulant expression for some time, it gets fixed and the expression becomes habitual. The hair may be trained to lie this way or that. These are examples of habit in living tissue. But there is one particular form of living tissue which is most susceptible to habit; that is nerve tissue. Let us review briefly the facts which underlie this characteristic. In nerve tissue, impressibility, conductivity and modifiability are developed to a marked degree. The nerve-cells in the sense organs are impressed by stimulations from the outside world. The nervous current thus generated is conducted over long nerve fibers, through the spinal cord to the brain where it is received and we experience a sensation. Thence it pushes on, over association neurones in the brain to motor neurones, over which it passes down the spinal cord again to muscles, and ends in some movement. In the pathway which it traverses it leaves its impression, and, thereafter, when the first neurone is excited, the nervous current tends to take the same pathway and to end in the same movement.

It should be emphasized that the nervous current, once started, always tends to seek outlet in movement. This is an extremely important feature of neural action, and, as will be shown in another chapter, is a vital factor in study. Movement may be started by the stimulation of a sense organ or by an idea. In the latter case it starts from regions in the brain without the immediately preceding stimulation of a sense organ. Howsoever it starts you may be sure that it seeks a way out, and prefers pathways already traversed. Hence you see you are bound to have habits. They will develop whether you wish them or not. Already you are "a bundle of habits"; they manifest themselves in two ways--as habits of action and habits of thought. You illustrate the first every time you tie your shoes or sign your name. To illustrate the second, I need only ask you to supply the end of this sentence: Columbus discovered America in----. Speech reveals many of these habits of thought. Certain phrases persist in the mind as habits so that when the phrase is once begun, you proceed habitually with the rest of it. When some one starts "in spite," your mind goes on to think "of"; "more or" calls up "less." When I ask you what word is called up by "black," you reply "white" according to the principles of mental habit. Your mind is arranged in such habitual patterns, and from these examples you readily see that a large part of what you do and think during the course of twenty-four hours is habitual. Twenty years hence you will be even more bound by this overpowering despot.

Our acts our angels are, or good, or ill, Our constant shadows that walk with us still.

Since you cannot avoid forming habits, how important it is that you seek to form those that are useful and desirable. In acquiring them, there are several general principles deducible from the facts of nervous action. The first is: Guard the pathways leading to the brain. Nerve tissue is impressible and everything that touches it leaves an ineradicable trace. You can control your habits to some extent, then, by observing caution in permitting things to impress you. Many unfortunate habits of study arise from neglect of this. The habit of using a "pony," for example, arises when one permits oneself to depend upon a group of English words in translating from a foreign language.

Nerve pathways should then be guarded with respect to *what* enters. They should also be guarded with respect to the *way* things enter. Remember, as the first pathway is cut, subsequent nervous currents will be directed. Consequently if you make a wrong pathway, you will have trouble undoing it.

Another maxim which will obviously prevent undesirable pathways is, go slowly at first. This is an important principle in all learning. If, when trying to learn the date 1453, you carelessly impress it first as 1435, you are likely to have trouble ever after in remembering which is right, 1453 or 1435. As you value your intellectual salvation, then, go slowly in making the first impression and be sure it is right. The next rule is: Guard the exits of the nervous currents. That is, watch the movements you make in response to impressions and ideas. This is necessary because the nervous current pushes on past obstructions, through areas in the brain, until it ends in some form of movement, and in finding the way out, it seeks those pathways that have been most frequently travelled. In study, it usually takes the form of movements of speech or writing. You will need to guard this part of the process just as you did the incoming pathway You must see that the movement is made which you wish to build into a habit. In learning the pronunciation of a foreign word, for example, see that your first pronunciation of it is absolutely right. When learning to typewrite see that you always hit the right key during the early trials. The point of exit of a nervous current is the point also where precautions are to be taken in developing good form. The path should be the shortest possible, involving only those muscles that are absolutely necessary. This makes for economy of effort.

The third general principle to be kept in mind is that habits are most easily formed in youth, for this is the period when nerve tissue is most easily impressed and modified. With respect to habit formation, then, you see that youth is the time when emphasis should be laid upon the formation of as many useful habits as possible. The world recognizes this to some extent and society is so organized that the youth of the race are given leisure and protection so that they may form useful habits. The world asks nothing of you during the next four years except that you develop yourself and form useful habits which will enable you in later life to take your place as a useful and stable member of society.

In addition to the principles just discussed, there are a number of other maxims which have been laid down as guides in the formation of new habits. The first is, *make an assertion of will.* Vow to yourself that you will form the habit, and keep that resolve ever before you.

The second maxim is, *make an emphatic start.* Surround yourself with every aid possible. Make it easy at first to perform the act and difficult not to perform it. For example, if you desire to form the habit of arising at six every morning, surround yourself with a number of aids. Buy an alarm clock, and tell some one of your decision. Such efforts at the start "will give your new beginning such a momentum that the temptation to break down will not occur as soon as it otherwise might; and every day during which a breakdown is postponed adds to the chances of its not occurring at all." Man has discovered the value of such devices during the course of his long history, and has evolved customs accordingly. When men decide to swear off smoking, they choose the opening of a new year when many other new things are being started; they make solemn promises to themselves, to each other, and finally to their friends. Such customs are precautions which help to bolster up the determination at the time when extraordinary effort and determination are required. In forming the habits incidental to college life, take pains from the start to surround yourself with as many aids as possible. This will not constitute a confession of weakness. It is only a wise and natural precaution which the whole experience of the race has justified. The third maxim is, _never permit an exception to occur_. Suppose you have a habit of saying "aint" which you wish to replace with a habit of saying "isn't." If the habit is deeply rooted, you have worn a pathway in the brain to a considerable depth, represented in the accompanying diagram by the line $A X B$.

A | X /\ B C

Let us suppose that you have already started the new habit, and have said the correct word ten times. That means you have worn another pathway $A X C$ to a considerable depth. During all this time, however, the old pathway is still open and at the slightest provocation will attract the nervous current. Your task is to deepen the new path so that the nervous current will flow into it instead of the old. Now suppose you make an exception on some occasion and allow the nervous current to travel over the old path. This unfortunate exception breaks down the bridge which you had constructed at *X* from *A* to *C*. But this is not the only result. The nervous current, as it revisits the old path, deepens it more than it was before, so the next time a similar situation arises, the current seeks the old path with much greater readiness than before, and vastly more effort is required to overcome it. Some one has likened the effect of these exceptions to that produced when one drops a ball of string that is partially wound. By a single slip, more is undone than can be accomplished in a dozen windings.

The fourth maxim is, _seize every opportunity to act upon your resolution_. The reason for this will be understood better if you keep in mind the fact, stated before, that nervous currents once started, whether from a sense-organ or from a brain-center, always tend to seek egress in movement. These outgoing nervous currents leave an imprint upon the modifiable nerve tissues as inevitably as do incoming impressions. Therefore, if you wish your resolves to be firmly fixed, you should act upon them speedily and often. "It is not in the moment of their forming, but in the moment of their producing *motor effects*, that resolves and aspirations communicate the new 'set' to the brain." "No matter how full a reservoir of *maxims* one may possess, and no matter how good one's *sentiments* may be, if one has not taken advantage of every concrete opportunity to *act*, one's character may remain entirely unaffected for the better." Particularly at time of emotional excitement one makes resolves that are very good, and a glow of fine feeling is present. Beware that these resolves do not evaporate in mere feeling. They should be crystallized in some form of action as soon as possible. "Let the expression be the least thing in the world--speaking genially to one's grandmother, or giving up one's seat in a ... car, if nothing more heroic offers--but let it not fail to take place." Strictly speaking you have not really completed a resolve until you have acted upon it. You may determine to go without lunch, but you have not consummated that resolve until you have permitted it to express itself by carrying you past the door of the dining-room. That is the crucial test which determines the strength of your resolve. Many repetitions will be required before a pathway is worn deep enough to be settled. Seize the very earliest opportunity to begin grooving it out, and seize every other opportunity for deepening it.

After this view of the place in your life occupied by habit, you readily see its far-reaching possibilities for welfare of body and mind. Its most obvious, because most annoying, effects are on the side of its disadvantages. Bad habits secure a grip upon us that we are sometimes powerless to shake off. True, this ineradicableness need have no terrors if we have formed good habits. Indeed, as will be pointed out in the next paragraph, habit may be a great asset. Nevertheless, it may work positive harm, or at best, may lead to stagnation. The fixedness of habit tends to make us move in ruts unless we exert continuous effort to learn new things. If we permit ourselves to move in old grooves we cease to progress and become "old fogy."

But the advantages of habit far outweigh its disadvantages. Habit helps the individual to be consistent and helps people to know what to expect from one. It helps society to be stable, to incorporate within itself modes of action conducive to the common good. For example, the respect which we all have for the property of others is a habit, and is so firmly intrenched that we should find ourselves unable to steal if we wished to. Habit is thus a very desirable asset and is truly called the "enormous fly-wheel of society."

A second advantage of habit is that it makes for accuracy. Acts that have become habitualized are performed more accurately than those not habitualized. Movements such as those made in typewriting and piano-playing, when measured in the psychological laboratory, are found to copy each other with extreme fidelity. The human body is a machine which may be adjusted to a high degree of nicety, and habit is the mechanism by which this adjustment is made.

A third advantage is that a stock of habits makes life easier. "There is no more miserable human being than one in whom nothing is habitual but indecision, for whom the lighting of every cigar, the drinking of every cup, the time of rising and going to bed every day and the beginning of every bit of work, are subjects of express volitional deliberation. Full half the time of such a man goes to the deciding or regretting of matters which ought to be so ingrained in him as practically not to exist for his consciousness at all." Have you ever reflected how miserable you would be and what a task living would be if you had to learn to write anew every morning when you go to class; or if you had to relearn how to tie your necktie every day? The burden of living would be intolerable.

The last advantage to be discerned in habit is economy. Habitual acts do not have to be actively directed by consciousness. While they are being performed, consciousness may be otherwise engaged. "The more of the details of our daily life we can hand over to the effortless custody of automatism, the more our higher powers of mind will be set free for their own proper work." While you are brushing your hair or tying your shoes, your mind may be engaged in memorizing poetry or calculating arithmetical problems. Habit is thus a great economizer.

The ethical consequences of habit are so striking that before leaving the subject we must give them acknowledgment. We can do no better than to turn to the statement by Professor James, whose wise remarks upon the subject have not been improved upon:

"The physiological study of mental conditions is thus the most powerful ally of hortatory ethics. The hell to be endured hereafter, of which theology tells, is no worse than the hell we make for ourselves in this world by habitually fashioning our characters in the wrong way. Could the young but realize how soon they will become mere walking bundles of habits, they would give more heed to their conduct while in the plastic state. We are spinning our own fates, good or evil, and never to be undone. Every smallest stroke of virtue or of vice leaves its never-so-little scar. The drunken Rip Van Winkle, in Jefferson's play, excuses himself for every fresh dereliction by saying, 'I won't count this time!' Well! he may not count it and a kind heaven may not count it; but it is being counted none the less. Down among his nerve-cells and fibers the molecules are counting it, registering it, and storing it up to be used against him when the next temptation comes. Nothing we ever do is, in strict scientific literalness, wiped out. Of course this has its good side as well as its bad one. As we become permanent drunkards by so many drinks, so we become saints in the moral, and authorities and experts in the practical and scientific, spheres, by so many separate acts and hours of work. But let no youth have any anxiety about the upshot of his education, whatever the line of it may be. If he keep faithfully busy each hour of the working day, he may safely leave the final result to itself. He can with perfect certainty count on waking up some fine morning, to find himself one of the competent ones of his generation, in whatever pursuit he has singled out. Silently, between all the details of his business, the _power of judging_ in all that class of matter will have built itself up within him as a possession that will never pass away. Young people should know the truth of this in advance. The ignorance of it has probably engendered more discouragement and faintheartedness in youths embarking on arduous careers than all other causes put together."

EXERCISE

Exercise 1. Point out an undesirable habit that you are determined to eradicate. Describe the desirable habit which you will adopt in its place. Give the concrete steps you will take in forming the new habit. How long a time do you estimate will be required for the formation of the new habit? Mark down the date and refer back to it when you have formed the habit, to see how accurately you estimated.

CHAPTER V

ACTIVE IMAGINATION

A very large part of the mental life of a student consists in the manipulation of images. By images we mean the revivals of things that have been impressed upon the senses. Call to mind for the moment your house-number as it appears upon the door of your home. In so doing you mentally reinstate something which has been impressed upon your senses many times; and you see it almost as clearly as if it were actually before you. The mental thing thus revived is called an image.

The word image is somewhat ill-chosen; for it usually signifies something connected with the eye, and implies that the stuff of mental images is entirely visual. The true fact of the matter is, we can image practically anything that we can sense. We may have tactual images of things touched; auditory images of things heard; gustatory images of things tasted; olfactory images of things smelled. How these behave in general and how they interact in study will engage our attention in this chapter.

The most highly dramatic use of images is in connection with that mental process known as Imagination. As we study the writings of Jack London, Poe, Defoe, Bunyan, we move in a realm almost wholly imaginary. And as we take a cross-section of our minds when thus engaged, we find them filled with images. Furthermore, they are of great variety--images of colors, sounds, tastes, smells, touches, even of sensations from our own internal organs, such as the palpitations of the heart that accompany feelings of pride, indignation, remorse, exaltation. A further characteristic is that they are sharp, clean-cut, vivid.

Note in the balcony scene from Romeo and Juliet, the number, variety and vividness of the images:

"But, soft! What light through yonder window breaks? It is the east, and Juliet is the sun. Arise, fair sun, and kill the envious moon, Who is already sick and pale with grief That thou, her maid, art far more fair than she. Be not her maid, since she is envious; Her vestal livery is but sick and green.... Two of the fairest stars in all the heaven, Having some business, do entreat her eyes To twinkle in their spheres till they return. What if her eyes were there, they in her head? The brightness in her cheek would shame those stars, As daylight doth a lamp; her eyes in heaven Would through the airy regions stream so bright That birds would sing and think it were not night. See, how she leans her cheek upon her hand! O, that I were a glove upon that hand, That I might touch that cheek!"

We may conclude, then, that three of the desirable attributes of great works of the imagination are *number, variety* and *vividness* of mental images.

One question that frequently arises concerning works of the imagination is, What is their source? Superficial thinkers have loosely answered, "Inspiration," implying, (according to the literal meaning of the word, "to breathe in"), that some mysterious external force (called by the ancients, "A Muse") enters into the mind of the author with a special revelation.

Psychological analysis of these imaginative works shows that this explanation is untrue. That the bizarre and apparently novel products arise from the experiences of the author, revived in imagination and combined in new ways. The horrendous incidents depicted in Dante's "Divine Comedy" never occurred within the lifetime experience of the author as such. Their separate elements did, however, and furnished the basis for Dante's clever combinations. The oft-heard saying that there is nothing new under the sun is psychologically true.

In the light of this brief analysis of products of the imagination we are ready to develop a program which we may follow in cultivating an active imagination.

Recognizing that images have their source in sensory experience, we see that the first step to take is to seek a multitude of experiences. Make intimate acquaintance with the objects of your environment. Handle them, tear them apart, put them together, place them next to other objects, noting the likenesses and differences. Thus you will acquire the stuff out of which images are made and will stock your mind with a number of images. Then when you wish to convey your ideas you will have a number of terms in which to do it--one of the characteristics of a free-flowing imagination.

The second characteristic we found to be variety. To secure this, seek a variety of sensational experiences. Perceive the objects of your experience through several senses--touch, smell, sight, hearing, taste. By means of this variety in sensations you will secure corresponding variety in your images.

To revive them easily sometimes requires practice. For it has been discovered that all people do not naturally call up images related to the various senses with equal ease. Most people use visual and auditory images more freely than they do other kinds. In order to develop skill in evoking the others, practise recalling them. Sit down for an hour of practice, as you would sit down for an hour of piano practice. Try to recall the taste of raisins, English walnuts; the smell of hyacinths, of witch-hazel; the rough touch of an orange-skin. Though you may at first have difficulty you will develop, with practice, a gratifying facility in recalling all varieties of images.

The third characteristic which we observed in works of the imagination is vividness. To achieve this, pay close attention to the details of your sensory experiences. Observe sharply the minute but characteristic items--the accent mark on *après*; the coarse stubby beard of the typical alley tough. Stock your mind with a wealth of such detailed impressions. Keep them alive by the kind of practice recommended in the preceding paragraph. Then describe the objects of your experience in terms of these significant details.

We discovered, in discussing the source of imaginative works, that the men whom we are accustomed to call imaginative geniuses do not have unique communication with heaven or with any external reservoir of ideas. Instead, we found their wonder-evoking creations to be merely new combinations of old images. The true secret of their success is their industrious utilization of past experiences according to the program outlined above. They select certain elements from their experiences and combine them in novel ways. This is the explanation of their strange, beautiful and bizarre productions. This is what Carlyle meant when he characterized genius as "the transcendent capacity for taking trouble" This is what Hogarth meant when he said, "Genius is nothing but labor and diligence." For concrete exemplification of this truth we need only turn to the autobiographies of great writers. In this passage from "John Barleycorn," Jack London describes his methods:

"Early and late I was at it--writing, typing, studying grammar, studying writing and all forms of writing, and studying the writers who succeeded in order to find out how they succeeded. I managed on five hours' sleep in the twenty-four, and came pretty close to working the nineteen waking hours left to me."

By saying that the novel effects of imagination come by way of industry, we do not mean to imply that one should strain after novelty and eccentricity. Unusual and happy combinations will come of themselves and naturally if one only makes a sufficient number.

There are laws of combination, known as the psychological laws of association, by which images will unite naturally. The number of possible combinations is infinite. By industriously making a large number, you will by the very laws of chance, stumble upon some that are especially happy and striking.

In summarizing this discussion, we may conclude that an active fertile imagination comes from crowding into one's life a large number of varied and vivid experiences; storing them up in the mind in the form of images; and industriously recalling and combining them in novel relationships. Mental images occur in other mental processes besides Imagination. They bulk importantly in memorizing, as we shall see in

Chapters

VI and VII; and in reasoning, as we shall see in Chapter IX. Throughout the book we shall find that as we develop ability to manipulate mental images, we shall increase the adaptability of all the mental processes.

READING AND EXERCISES

Reading: Dearborn (2) Chapter III.

Exercise 1. Call up in imagination the sound of your French instructor's voice as he says *étudiant*. Call up the appearance on the page of the conjugation of *être*, present tense.

Exercise 2. Choose some word which you have had difficulty in learning. Look at it attentively, securing a perfectly clear impression of it; then practise calling up the visual image of it, until you secure perfect reproduction.

Exercise 3. List the different images called up by the passage from *Romeo and Juliet*.

CHAPTER VI

FIRST AIDS TO MEMORY; IMPRESSION

Of all the mental operations employed by the student, memory is probably the one in which the greatest inefficiency is manifested. Though we often fail to realize it, much of our life is taken up with memorizing. Every time we make use of past experience, we rely upon this function of the mind, but in no occupation is it quite so practically important as in study. We shall begin our investigation of memory by dividing it into four phases or stages--Impression, Retention, Recall and Recognition. Any act of memory involves them all. There is first a stage when the material is being impressed; second, a stage when it is being retained so that it may be revived in the future; third, a stage of recall when the retained material is revived to meet present needs; fourth, a feeling of recognition, through which the material is recognized as having previously been in the mind.

Impression is accomplished through the sense organs; and in the foregoing chapter we laid down the rule: Guard the avenues of impression and admit only such things as you wish to retain. This necessitates that you go slowly at first. This is a principle of all habit formation, but is especially important in habits of memorizing. Much of the poor memory that people complain about is due to the fact that they make first impressions carelessly. One reason why people fail to remember names is that they do not get a clear impression of the name at the start. They are introduced in a hurry or the introducer mumbles; consequently no clear impression is secured. Under such circumstances how could one expect to retain and recall the name? Go slowly, then, in impressing material for the first time. As you look up the words of a foreign language in the lexicon, trying to memorize their English equivalents, take plenty of time. Obtain a clear impression of the sound and appearance of the words.

Inasmuch as impressions may be made through any of the sense organs, one problem in the improvement of memory concerns the choice of sense avenues. As an infant you used all senses impartially in your eager search after information. You voraciously put things into your mouth and discovered that some things were sweet, some sour. You bumped your head against things and learned that some were hard and some soft. In your insatiable curiosity you pulled things apart and peered into them; in short, utilized all the sense organs. In adult life, however, and in education as it takes place through the agency of books and instructors, most learning depends upon the eye and ear. Even yet, however, you learn many things through the sense of touch and through muscle movement, though you may be unaware of it. You probably have better success retaining impressions made upon one sense than another. The majority of people retain better things that are visually impressed. Such persons think often in terms of visual images. When thinking of water running from a faucet, they can see the water fall, see it splash, but have no trace of the sound. The whole event is noiseless in memory. When they think of their instructor, they can see him standing at his desk but cannot imagine the sound of his voice. When striving to think of the causes leading to the Civil War, they picture them as they are listed on the page of the text-book or note-book. Other people have not this ability to recall in visual terms, but depend to greater extent upon sounds. When asked to think about their instructor, they do it in terms of his voice. When asked to conjugate a French verb, they hear it pronounced mentally but do not see it on the page. These are extremes of imagery type, but they illustrate preferences as they are found in many persons. Some persons use all senses with ease; others unconsciously work out combinations, preferring one sense for some kinds of material and another for other kinds. For example, one might prefer visual impression for remembering dates in history but auditory impression for conjugating French verbs. You will find it profitable to examine yourself and discover your preferences. If you find that you have greater difficulty in remembering material impressed through the ear than through the eye, reduce things to visual terms as much as possible. Make your lecture notes more complete or tabulate things that you wish to remember, thus securing impression from the written form. The writer has difficulty in remembering names that are only heard. So he asks that the name be spelled, then projects the letters on an imaginary background, thus forming visual stuff which can easily be recalled. If, on the contrary, you remember best the things that you hear, you may find it a good plan to read your lessons aloud. Many a student, upon the discovery of such a preference, has increased his memory ability many fold by adopting the simple expedient of reading his lessons aloud. It might be pointed out that while you are reading aloud, you are making more than auditory impressions. By the use of the vocal organs you are making muscular impressions, which also aid in learning, as will be pointed out in

Chapter X.

After this discussion do not jump to the conclusion that just because you find some difficulty in using one sense avenue for impression, it is therefore impossible to develop it. Facility in using particular senses can be gained by practice. To improve ability to form visual images of things, practise calling up visions of things. Try to picture a page of your history textbook. Can you see the headlines of the sections and the paragraphs? To develop auditory imagery, practise calling up sounds. Try to image your French instructor's voice in saying *élève*. The development of these sense fields is a slow and laborious process and one questions whether it is worth while for a student to undertake the labor involved when another sense is already very efficient. Probably it is most economical to Arrange impressions so as to favor the sense that is already well developed and reliable.

Another important condition of impression is repetition. It is well known that material which is repeated several times is remembered more easily than that impressed but once. If two repetitions induce a given liability to recall, four or eight will secure still greater liability of recall. Your knowledge of brain action makes this rule intelligible, because you know the pathway is deepened every time the nervous current passes over it.

Experiments in the psychological laboratory have shown that it is best in making impressions to make more than enough impressions to insure recall. "If material is to be retained for any length of time, a simple mastery of it for immediate recall is not sufficient. It should be learned far beyond the point of immediate reproduction if time and energy are to be saved." This principle of learning points out the fact that there are two kinds of memory--immediate and deferred. The first kind involves recall immediately after impression is made; the second involves recall at some later time. It is a well-known fact that things learned a long time before they are to be recalled fade away. If you are not going to recall material until a long time after the impression, store up enough impressions so that you can afford to lose a few and still retain enough until time for recall. Another reason for "overlearning" is that when the time comes for recall you are likely to be disturbed. If it is a time of public performance, you may be embarrassed; or you may be hurried or under distractions. Accordingly you should have the material exceedingly well memorized so that these distractions will not prove detrimental.

The mere statement made above, that repetition is necessary in impression, is not sufficient. It is important to know how to distribute the repetitions. Suppose you are memorizing "Psalm of Life" to be recited a month from to-day, and that you require thirty repetitions of the poem to learn it. Shall you make these thirty repetitions at one sitting? Or shall you distribute them among several sittings? In general, it is better to spread the repetitions over a period of time. The question then arises, what is the most effective distribution? Various combinations are possible. You might rehearse the poem once a day during the month, or twice a day for the first fifteen days, or the last fifteen days, four times every fourth day, _ad infinitum_. In the face of these possibilities is there anything that will guide us in distributing the repetitions? We shall get some light on the question from an examination of the curve of forgetting--a curve that has been plotted showing the rate at which the mind tends to forget. Forgetting proceeds according to law, the curve descending rapidly at first and then more slowly. "The larger proportion of the material learned is forgotten the first day or so. After that a constantly decreasing amount is forgotten on each succeeding day for perhaps a week, when the amount remains practically stationary." This gives us some indication that the early repetitions should be closer together than those at the end of the period. So long as you are forgetting rapidly you will need more repetitions in order to counterbalance the tendency to forget. You might well make five repetitions; then rest. In about an hour, five more; within the next twenty-four hours, five more. By this time you should have the poem memorized, and all within two days. You would still have fifteen repetitions of the thirty, and these might be used in keeping the poem fresh in the mind by a repetition every other day.

As intimated above, one important principle in memorizing is to make the first impressions as early as possible, for older impressions have many chances of being retained. This is evidenced by the vividness of childhood scenes in the minds of our grandparents. An old soldier recalls with great vividness events that happened during the Civil War, but forgets events of yesterday. There is involved here a principle of nervous action that you have already encountered; namely, that impressions are more easily made and retained in youth. It should also be observed that pathways made early have more chances of being used than those made recently. Still another peculiarity of nervous action is revealed in these extended periods of memorizing. It has been discovered that if a rest is taken between impressions, the impressions become more firmly fixed. This points to the presence of a surprising power, by which we are able to learn, as it were, while we sleep. We shall understand this better if we try to imagine what is happening in the nervous system. Processes of nutrition are constantly going on. The blood brings in particles to repair the nerve cells, rebuilding them according to the pattern left by the last impression. Indeed, the entrance of this new material makes the impression even more fixed. The nutritional processes seem to set the impression much as a hypo bath fixes or sets an impression on a photographic plate. This peculiarity of memory led Professor James to suggest, paradoxically, that we learn to skate in summer and to swim in winter. And, indeed, one usually finds, in beginning the skating season, that after the initial stiffness of muscles wears off, one glides along with surprising agility. You see then that if you plan things rightly, Nature will do much of your learning for you. It might be suggested that perhaps things impressed just before going to sleep have a better chance to "set" than things impressed at other times for the reason that sleep is the time when the reparative processes of the body are most active.

Since the brain pattern requires time to "set," it is important that after the first impression you refrain from introducing anything immediately into the mind that might disturb it. After you have impressed the poem you are memorizing, do not immediately follow it by another poem. Let the brain rest for three or four minutes until after the first impressions have had a chance to "set."

Now that we have regarded this "unconscious memorizing" from the neurological standpoint, let us consider it from the psychological standpoint. How are the ideas being modified during the intervals between impressions? Modern psychology has discovered that much memorizing goes on without our knowing it, paradoxical as that may seem. The processes may be described in terms of the doctrine of association, which is that whenever two things have once been associated together in the mind, there is a tendency thereafter "if the first of them recurs, for the other to come with it." After the poem of our illustration has once been repeated, there is a tendency for events in everyday experience that are like it to associate themselves with it. For example, in the course of a day or week many things might arise and recall to you the line, "Life is real, life is earnest", and it would become, by that fact, more firmly fixed in the mind. This valuable semi-conscious recall requires that you must make the first impression as early as possible before the time for ultimate recall. This persistence of ideas in the mind means "that the process of learning does not cease with the actual work of learning, but that, if not disturbed, this process runs on of itself for a time, and adds a little to the result of our labors. It also means that, if it is to our advantage to stand in readiness with some word or thought, we shall be able to do so, if only this word or thought recur to us but once, some time before the critical moment. So we remember to keep a promise to pay a call, to make a remark at the proper time, even though we turn our mind to other work or talk for some hours between. We can do this because, if not vigorously prevented, ideas and words keep on reappearing in the mind." You may utilize this principle in theme-writing to good advantage. As soon as the instructor announces the subject for a theme, begin to think about it. Gather together all the ideas you have about the subject and start your mind to work upon it. Suppose you take as a theme-subject The Value of Training in Public Speaking for a Business Man. The first time this is suggested to you, a few thoughts, at least, will come to you. Write them down, even though they are disconnected and heterogeneous. Then as you go about your other work you will find a number of occasions that will arouse ideas bearing upon this subject. You may read in a newspaper of a brilliant speech made before the Chamber of Commerce by a leading business man, which will serve as an illustration to support your affirmative position; or you may attend a banquet where a prominent business man disappoints his audience with a wretched speech. Such experiences, and many others, bearing more or less directly upon the subject, will come to you, and will call up the theme-subject, with which they will unite themselves. Write down these ideas as they occur, and you will find that when you start to compose the theme formally, it almost writes itself, requiring for the most part only expansion and arrangement of ideas. While thus organizing the theme you will reap even more benefits from your early start, for, as you are composing it, you will find new ideas crowding in upon you which you did not know you possessed, but which had been associating themselves in your mind with this topic even when you were unaware of the fact.

In writing themes, the principle of distribution of time may also be profitably employed. After you have once written a theme, lay it aside for a while--perhaps a week. Then when you take it up, read it in a detached manner and you will note many places where it may be improved. These benefits are to be enjoyed only when a theme is planned a long time ahead. Hence the rule to start as early as possible.

Before leaving the subject of theme-writing, which was called up by the discussion of unconscious memory, another suggestion will be given that may be of service to you. When correcting a theme, employ more than one sense avenue. Do not simply glance over it with your eye. Read it aloud, either to yourself or, better still, to someone else. When you do this you will be amazed to discover how different it sounds and what a new view you secure of it. When you thus change your method of composition, you will find a new group of ideas thronging into your mind. In the auditory rendition of a theme you will discover faults of syntax which escaped you in silent reading. You will note duplication of words, split infinitives, mixed tenses, poorly balanced sentences. Moreover, if your mind has certain peculiarities, you may find even more advantages accruing from such a practice. The author, for example, has a slightly different set of ideas at his disposal according to the medium of expression employed. When writing with a pencil, one set of ideas comes to mind; with a typewriter slightly different ideas arise; when talking to an audience, still different ideas. Three sets of ideas and three vocabularies are thus available for use on any subject. In adopting this device of composing through several mediums, you should combine with it the principle of distributing time already discussed in connection with repetition of impressions. Write a theme one day, then lay it aside for a few days and go back to it with a fresh mind. The rests will be found very beneficial in helping you to get a new viewpoint of the subject.

Reverting to our discussion of memory, we come upon another question: In memorizing material like the poem of our example, should one impress the entire poem at once, or break it up into parts, impressing a stanza each day? Most people would respond, without thought, the latter, and, as a matter of fact, most memorizing takes place in this way. Experimental psychology, however, has discovered that this is uneconomical. The selection, if of moderate length, should be impressed as a whole. If too long for this, it should be broken up as little as possible. In order to see the necessity for this let us examine your experiences with the memorization of poems in your early school days. You probably proceeded as follows: After school one day, you learned the first stanza, then went out to play. The next day you learned the second one, and so on. You thought at the end of a week that you had memorized it because, at the end of each day's sitting, you were able to recite perfectly the stanza learned that day. On "speaking day" you started out bravely and recited the first stanza without mishap. When you started to think of the second one, however, it would not come. The memory balked. Now what was the matter? How can we explain this distressing blank? In psychological terms, we ascribe the difficulty to the failure to make proper associations between stanzas. Association was made effectively between the lines of the single stanzas, but not between the separate stanzas. After you finished impressing the first stanza, you went about something else; playing ball, perhaps. When you approached the poem the next day you started in with the second stanza. There was then no bridge between the two. There was nothing to link the last line of the first stanza,

"And things are not what they seem,"

with the first line of the next stanza,

"Life is real, life is earnest."

This makes clear the necessity of impressing the poem as a whole instead of by parts.

According to another classification, there are two ways of memorizing--by rote and by logical associations. Rote memorizing involves the repetition of material just as it stands, and usually requires such long and laborious drill that it is seldom economical. True, some matter must be memorized this way; such as the days of the week and the names of the months; but there is another and gentler method which is usually more effective and economical than that of brutal repetition. That is the method of logical association, by which one links up a new fact with something already in the mind. If, for example, you wish to remember the date of the World's Fair in Chicago, you might proceed as follows: Ask yourself, What did the Fair commemorate? The discovery of America in 1492, the four hundredth anniversary occurring in 1892. The Fair could not be made ready in that year, however, so was postponed a year. Such a process of memorizing the date is less laborious than the method of rote memory, and is usually more likely to lead to ready recall. The old fact already in mind acts as a magnet which at some later time may call up other facts that had once been associated with it. You can easily see that this new fact might have been associated with several old facts, thus securing more chances of being called up. From this it may be inferred that the more facts you have in your mind about a subject the more chances you have of retaining new facts. It is sometimes thought that if a person stores so much in his memory it will soon be so full that he cannot memorize any more. This is a false notion, involving a conception of the brain as a hopper into which impressions are poured until it runs over. On the contrary, it should be regarded as an interlacing of fibers with infinite possibilities of inter-connection, and no one ever exhausts the number of associations that can be made.

The method of logical association may be employed with telling effect in the study of foreign languages. When you meet a new word scrutinize it carefully for some trace of a word already familiar to you either in that language or in another. This independent discovery of meanings is a very great aid in saving time and in fixing the meaning of new words. Opportunities for this method are especially frequent in the German language, since so many German words are formed by compounding other words. "Rathausmarkt" is a long and apparently difficult German word, and one's first temptation is to look it up in the lexicon and promptly forget it. Let us analyze it, however, and we shall see that it is only a compound of already familiar words. "*Rat*" is already familiar as the word for counsel ("*raten*" to give advice); "*haus*" is equally familiar. So we see that the first part of the word means council-house; the council-house of a city is called a city hall. "*Markt*" is equally familiar as market-square, so the significance of the entire word stands, city-hall-square. By such a method of utilizing facts already known, you may make yourself much more independent of the lexicon and may make your memory for foreign words much more tenacious.

We approach a phase of impression the importance of which is often unsuspected; namely, the intention with which memorizing is done. The fidelity of memory is greatly affected by the intention. If, at the time of impression, you intend to retain only until the time of recall, the material tends to slip away after that time. If, however, you impress with the intention to retain permanently the material stays by you better. Students make a great mistake when they study for the purpose merely of retaining until after examination time. Intend to retain facts permanently, and there will be greater likelihood of their permanence.

READINGS AND EXERCISES

Readings: Adams (1) Chapter III. Seashore (16) Chapter II. Swift (20)

Chapter VII.

Watt (21).

Exercise I. Cite examples from your own experience showing the effects of the following faults in making impressions. *a.* First impression not clear. *b.* Insufficient number of repetitions. *c.* Use of rote method instead of method of logical association. *d.* Impressions not distributed. *e.* Improper use of "part" method.

Exercise 2. After experimentation, state what is your most effective sense avenue for the impression of foreign words, facts in history, the pronunciation of English words.

Exercise 3. Make a preliminary draft of your next theme; lay it aside for a day or two; then write another on the same subject; combine the two, using the best parts of each; lay this aside for a day or two; then read it aloud, making such changes as are prompted by the auditory presentation. Can you find elements of worth in this method, which will warrant you in adopting it, at least, in part?

CHAPTER VII

SECOND AIDS TO MEMORY: RETENTION, RECALL AND RECOGNITION

Our discussion up to this point has centred around the phase of memory called impression. We have described some of the conditions favorable to impression and have seen that certain and accurate memory depends upon adherence to them. The next phase of memory--Retention--cannot be described in psychological terms. We know we retain facts after they are once impressed, but as to their status in the mind we can say nothing. If you were asked when the Declaration of Independence was signed, you would reply instantly. When asked, however, where that fact was five minutes ago, you could not answer. Somewhere in the recesses of the mind, perhaps, but as to immediate awareness of it, there was none. We may try to think of retention in terms of nerve cells and say that at the time when the material was first impressed there was some modification made in certain nerve cells which persisted. This trait of nerve modifiability is one factor which accounts for greater retentive power in some persons than in others. It must not be concluded, however, that all good memory is due to the inheritance of this trait. It is due partly to observance of proper conditions of impression, and much can be done to overcome or offset innate difficulty of modification by such observance.

We are now ready to examine the third phase of memory--Recall. This is the stage at which material that has been impressed and retained is recalled to serve the purpose for which it was memorized. Recall is thus the goal of memory, and all the devices so far discussed have it for their object. Can we facilitate recall by any other means than by faithful and intelligent impressions? For answer let us examine the state of mind at time of recall.

We find that it is a unique mental state. It differs from impression in being a period of more active search for facts in the mind accompanied by expression, instead of a concentration upon the external impression. It is also usually accompanied by motor expressions, either talking or writing. Since recall is a unique mental state, you ought to prepare for it by means of a rehearsal. When you are memorizing anything to be recalled, make part of your memorizing a rehearsal of it, if possible, under same conditions as final recall. In memorizing from a book, first make impression, then close the book and practise recall. When memorizing a selection to be given in a public speaking class, intersperse the periods of impression with periods of recall. This is especially necessary in preparation for public speaking, for facing an audience gives rise to a vastly different psychic attitude from that of impression. The sight of an audience may be embarrassing or exciting. Furthermore, unforeseen distractions may arise. Accordingly, create those conditions as nearly as possible in your preparation. Imagine yourself facing the audience. Practise aloud so that you will become accustomed to the sound of your own voice. The importance of the practice of recall as a part of the memory process can hardly be overestimated. One psychologist has advised that in memorizing significant material more than half the time should be spent in practising recall.

There still remains a fourth phase of memory--Recognition. Whenever a remembered fact is recalled, it is accompanied by a characteristic feeling which we call the feeling of recognition. It has been described as a feeling of familiarity, a glow of warmth, a sense of ownership, a feeling of intimacy. As you walk down the street of a great city you pass hundreds of faces, all of them strange. Suddenly in the crowd you catch sight of some one you know and are instantly suffused with a glow of feeling that is markedly different from your feeling toward the others. That glow represents the feeling of recognition. It is always present during recall and may be used in great advantage in studying. It derives its virtue for our purpose from the fact that it is a feeling, and at the time of feeling the bodily activities in general are affected. Changes occur in heart beat, breathing; various glandular secretions are affected, the digestive organs respond. In this general quickening of bodily activity we have reason to believe that the nervous system partakes, and things become impressed more readily. Thus the feeling of recognition that accompanies recall is responsible for one of the benefits of reviews. At such a time material once memorized becomes tinged with a feelingful color different from that which accompanied it when new. Review, then, not merely to produce additional impressions, but also to take advantage of the feeling of recognition.

We have now discussed memory in its four phases and have seen clearly that it operates not in a blind, chaotic manner, but according to law. Certain conditions are required and when they are met memory is good. After providing proper conditions for memory, then, trust your memory. An attitude of confidence is very necessary. If, when you are memorizing, you continually tremble for fear that you will not recall at the desired moment, the fixedness of the impression will be greatly hindered. Therefore, after utilizing all your knowledge about the conditions of memorizing, rest content and trust to the laws of Nature. They will not fail you.

By this time you have seen that memory is not a mysterious mental faculty with which some people are generously endowed, and of which others are deprived. All people of normal intelligence can remember and can improve their ability if they desire. The improvement does not take the form that some people expect, however. No magic wand can transform you into a good memorizes You must work the transformation yourself. Furthermore, it is not an instantaneous process to be accomplished overnight. It will come about only after you have built up a set of habits, according to our conception of study as a process of habit formation.

A final word of caution should be added. Some people think of memory as a separate division or compartment of the mind which can be controlled and improved by exercising it alone. Such a conception is fallacious. Improvement in memory will involve improvement in other mental abilities, and you will find that as you improve your ability to remember, you will develop at the same time better powers to concentrate attention, to image, to associate facts and to reason.

READING AND EXERCISE

Reading: See readings for Chapter VI.

Exercise I. Compare the mental conditions of impression with those of recall.

CHAPTER VIII

CONCENTRATION OF ATTENTION

Nearly everyone has difficulty in the concentration of attention. Brain workers in business and industry, students in high school and college, and even professors in universities, complain of the same difficulty. Attention seems in some way to be at the very core of mental activity, for no matter from what aspect we view the mind, its excellence seems to depend upon the power to concentrate attention. When we examine a growing infant, one of the first signs by which we judge the awakening of intelligence is the power to pay attention or to "notice things." When we examine the intellectual ability of normal adults we do so by means of tests that require close concentration of attention. In judging the intelligence of people with whom we associate every day, we regard one who is able to maintain close attention for long periods of time as a person of strong mind. We rate Thomas Edison as a powerful thinker when we read that he becomes so absorbed in work that he neither eats nor sleeps. Finally, when we examine the insane and the feeble-minded, we find that one form which their derangements take is an inability to control the attention. This evidence, added to our own experience, shows us the importance of concentration of attention in study and we become even more desirous of investigating attention to see how we may develop it.

We shall be better able to discuss attention if we select for analysis a concrete situation when the mind is in a state of concentrated attention. Concentrate for a moment upon the letter O. Although you are ostensibly focussing all your powers of attention upon the letter, nevertheless you are really aware of a number of things besides: of other words on the page; of other objects in the field of vision; of sounds in the room and on the street; of sensations from your clothing; and of sensations from your bodily organs, such as the heart and lungs. In addition to these sensations, you will find, if you introspect carefully enough, that your mind also contains a number of ideas and imaginings; thoughts about the paragraph you just read or about one of your lessons. Thus we see that at a time when we apparently focus our attention upon but one thing, we really have a large number of things in our mind, and they are of a great variety. The mental field might be represented by a circle, at the centre of which is the object of attention. It may be an object in the external world perceived through one of the senses, or it may be an idea we are thinking about, such, for example, as the idea of infinity. But whether the thing attended to is a perception or an idea, we may properly speak of it as the object of attention or the "focal" object. In addition to this, we must recognize the presence of a large number of other objects, both sensory and ideational. These are nearer the margin of the mental field, so we call them "marginal."

The distinctive thing about a state of mind such as that just described is that the focal object is much clearer than the marginal objects. For example, when you fixated the letter O, it was only in the vaguest sort of fashion that you were aware of the contact of your clothing or the lurking ideas of other lessons. As we examine these marginal objects further, we find that they are continually seeking to crowd into the centre of attention and to become clear. You may be helped in forming a vivid picture of conditions if you think of the mind as a stream ever in motion, and as it flows on, the objects in it continually shift their positions. A cross-section of the stream at any moment may show the contents of the mind arranged in a particular pattern, but at the very next moment they may be arranged in a different pattern, another object occupying the focus, while the previous tenant is pushed to the margin. Thus we see that it is a tendency of the mind to be forever changing. If left to itself, it would be in ceaseless fluctuation, the whim of every passing fancy. This tendency to fluctuate comes with more or less regularity, some psychologists say every second or two. True, we do not always yield to the fluctuating tendency, nevertheless we are recurrently tempted, and we must exercise continuous effort to keep a particular object at the focus. The power to exert effort and to regulate the arrangement of our states of mind is the peculiar gift of man, and is a prime function of education. Viewed in this light, then, we see that the voluntary focusing of our attention consists in the selecting of certain objects to be attended to, and the ignoring of other objects which act as distractions. We may conveniently classify the latter as external sensations, bodily sensations and irrelevant ideas.

Let us take an actual situation that may arise in study and see how this applies. Suppose you are in your room studying about Charlemagne, a page of your history text occupying the centre of your attention. The marginal distractions in such a case would consist, first, in external sensations, such as the glare from your study-lamp, the hissing of the radiator, the practising of a neighboring vocalist, the rattle of passing street-cars. The bodily distractions might consist of sensations of weariness referred to the back, the arms and the eyes, and fainter sensations from the digestive organs, heart and lungs. The irrelevant ideas might consist of thoughts about a German lesson which you are going to study, visions of a face, or thoughts about some social engagement. These marginal objects are in the mind even when you conscientiously focus your mind upon the history lesson, and, though vague, they try to force their way into the focus and become clear. The task of paying attention, then, consists in maintaining the desired object at the centre of the mental field and keeping the distractions away. With this definition of attention, we see that in order to increase the effectiveness of attention during study, we must devise means for overcoming the distractions peculiar to study. Obviously the first thing is to eliminate every distraction possible. Such a plan of elimination may require a radical rearrangement of study conditions, for students often fail to realize how wretched their conditions of study are from a psychological standpoint. They attempt to study in rooms with two or three others who talk and move about continually; they drop down in any spot in the library and expose themselves needlessly to a great number of distractions. If you wish to become a good student, you must prepare conditions as favorable as possible for study. Choose a quiet room to live in, free from distracting sounds and sights. Have your room at a temperature neither too hot nor too cold; 68° F. is usually considered favorable for study. When reading in the library, sit down in a quiet spot, with your back to the door, so you will not be tempted to look up as people enter the room. Do not sit near a group of gossipers or near a creaking door. Having made the external conditions favorable for study, you should next address yourself to the task of eliminating bodily distractions. The most disturbing of these in study are sensations of fatigue, for, contrary to the opinion of many people, study is very fatiguing work and involves continual strain upon the muscles in holding the body still, particularly those of the back, neck, arms, hands and, above all, the eyes. How many movements are made by your eyes in the course of an hour's study! They sweep back and forth across the page incessantly, being moved by six muscles which are bound to become fatigued. Still more fatigue comes from the contractions of delicate muscles within the eyeball, where adjustments are made for far and near vision and for varying amounts of light. The eyes, then, give rise to much fatigue, and, altogether, are the source of a great many bodily distractions in study.

Other distractions may consist of sensations from the clothing. We are always vaguely aware of pressure of our clothing. Usually it is not sufficiently noticeable to cause much annoyance, but occasionally it is, as is demonstrated at night when we take off a shoe with such a sigh of relief that we realize in retrospect it had been vaguely troubling us all day.

In trying to create conditions for efficient study, many bodily distractions can be eliminated. The study chair should be easy to sit in so as to reduce fatigue of the muscles supporting the body; the book-rest should be arranged so as to require little effort to hold the book; the light should come over the left shoulder. This is especially necessary in writing, so that the writing hand will not cast a shadow upon the work. The muscles of the eyes will be rested and fatigue will be retarded if you close the eyes occasionally. Then in order to lessen the general fatigue of the body, you may find it advantageous to rise and walk about occasionally. Lastly, the clothing should be loose and unconfining; especially should there be plenty of room for circulation.

In the overcoming of distractions, we have seen that much may be done by way of eliminating distractions, and we have pointed out the way to accomplish this to a certain extent. But in spite of our most careful provisions, there will still be distractions that cannot be eliminated. You cannot, for example, chloroform the vocalist in the neighboring apartment, nor stop the street-cars while you study; you cannot rule out fatigue sensations entirely, and you cannot build a fence around the focus of your mind so as to keep out unwelcome and irrelevant ideas. The only thing to do then is to accept as inevitable the presence of some distractions, and to realise that to pay attention, it is necessary to habituate yourself to the ignoring of distractions.

In the accomplishment of this end it will be necessary to apply the principles of habit formation already described. Start out by making a strong determination to ignore all distractions. Practise ignoring them, and do not let a slip occur. Try to develop interest in the object of attention, because we pay attention to those things in which we are most interested. A final point that may help you is to use the first lapse of attention as a reminder of the object you desire to fixate upon. This may be illustrated by the following example: Suppose, in studying a history lesson, you come upon a reference to the royal apparel of Charlemagne. The word "royal" might call up purple, a Northwestern University pennant, the person who gave it to you, and before you know it you are off in a long day-dream leading far from the history lesson. Such migrations as these are very likely to occur in study, and constitute one of the most treacherous pitfalls of student life. In trying to avoid them, you must form habits of disregarding irrelevant ideas when they try to obtrude themselves. And the way to do this is to school yourself so that the first lapse of attention will remind you of the lesson in hand. It can be done if you keep yourself sensitive to wanderings of attention, and let the first slip from the topic with which you are engaged remind you to pull yourself back. Do this before you have taken the step that will carry you far away, for with each step in the series of associations it becomes harder to draw yourself back into the correct channel.

In reading, one frequent cause for lapses of attention and for the intrusion of unwelcome ideas is obscurity in the material being read. If you trace back your lapses of attention, you will often find that they first occur when the thought becomes difficult to follow, the sentence ambiguous, or a single word unusual. As a result, the meaning grows hazy in your mind and you fail to comprehend it. Naturally, then, you drift into a channel of thought that is easier to follow. This happens because the mental stream tends to seek channels of least resistance. If you introspect carefully, you will undoubtedly discover that many of your annoying lapses of attention can be traced to such conditions. The obvious remedy is to make sure that you understand everything as you read. As soon as you feel the thought growing difficult to follow, begin to exert more effort; consult the dictionary for the meanings of words you do not understand. Probably the ordinary freshman in college ought to look up the meaning of as many as twenty words daily.

Again, the thought may be difficult to follow because your previous knowledge is deficient; perhaps the discussion involves some fact which you never did comprehend clearly, and you will naturally fail to understand something built upon it. If deficiency of knowledge is the cause of your lapses of attention, the obvious remedy is to turn back and study the fundamental facts; to lay a firm foundation in your subjects of study.

This discussion shows that the conditions at time of concentrated attention are very complex; that the mind is full of a number of things; that your object as a student is to keep some one thing at the focus of your mind, and that in doing so you must continuously ignore other mental contents. In our psychological descriptions we have implied that the mind stands still at times, permitting us to take a cross-section and examine it minutely. As a matter of fact, the mind never stands still. It continually moves along, and at no two moments is it exactly the same. This results in a condition whereby an idea which is at one moment at the centre cannot remain there unless it takes on a slightly different appearance from moment to moment. When you attempted to fix your attention upon the letter O, you found a constant tendency to shift the attention, perhaps to a variation in the intensity of the type or to a flaw in the type or in the paper. In view of the inevitable nature of these changes, you see that in spite of your best efforts you cannot expect to maintain any object of study inflexibly at the centre of attention. The way to do is to manipulate the object so that it will appear from moment to moment in a slightly different light. If, for example, you are trying to concentrate upon a rule of English grammar long enough to memorize it, do not read it over and over again, depending solely upon repetition. A better way, after thoroughly comprehending it, is to think about it in several relations; compare it with other rules, noting points of likeness and difference; apply it to the construction of a sentence. The essential thing is to do something with it. Only thus can you keep it in the focus of attention. This is equivalent to the restatement of another fact stressed in a previous chapter, namely, that the mind is not a passive thing that stands still, but an active thing. When you give attention, you actively select from a number of possible objects one to be clearer than the rest. This selection requires effort under most conditions of study, but you may be cheered by the thought that as you develop interest in the fields of study, and as you develop habits of ignoring distractions, you will be able to fixate your attention with less and less effort. A further important fact is that as you develop power to select objects for the consideration of attention, you develop simultaneously other mental processes--the ability to memorize, to economize time and effort and to control future thoughts and actions. In short, power to concentrate attention means power in all the mental processes.

EXERCISES

Exercise I. "Watch a small dot so far away that it can just be seen. Can you see it all the time? How many times a minute does it come and go?" Make what inference you can from this regarding the fluctuation of attention during study.

Exercise 2. What concrete steps will you take in order to accommodate your study to the fluctuations of attention?

Exercise 3. The next time you have a lapse of attention during study, retrace your steps of thought, write down the ideas from the last one in your mind to the one which started the digression. Represent the digression graphically if you can.

Exercise 4. Make a list of the things that most persistently distract your attention during study. What specific steps will you take to eliminate them; to ignore the unavoidable ones?

CHAPTER IX

HOW WE REASON

If you were asked to describe the most embarrassing of your class-room experiences, you would probably cite the occasions when the instructor asks you a series of questions demanding close reasoning. As he pins you down to statement of facts and forces you to draw valid conclusions, you feel in a most perplexed frame of mind. Either you find yourself unable to give reasons, or you entangle yourself in contradictions. In short, you flounder about helplessly and feel as though the bottom of your ship of knowledge has dropped out. And when the ordeal is over and you have made a miserable botch of a recitation which you thought you had been perfectly prepared for, you complain that "if the instructor had followed the book," or "if he had asked straight questions," you would have answered every one perfectly, having memorized the lesson "word for word."

This complaint, so often voiced by students, reveals the fundamental characteristic which distinguishes the mental operation of reasoning from the others we have studied. In reasoning we face a new kind of situation presenting difficulties not encountered in the simpler processes of sensation, memory, and imagery, and when we attempt to substitute these simple processes for reasoning, we fail miserably, for the two kinds of processes are essentially different, and cannot be substituted one for the other.

Broadly speaking, the mental activities of study may be divided into two groups, which, for want of better names, we shall call processes of acquisition and processes of construction. The mental attitude of the first is that of acquirement. "Sometimes our main business seems to be to acquire knowledge; certain matters are placed before us in books or by our teachers, and we are required to master them, to make them part of our stock of knowledge. At other times we are called upon to use the knowledge we already possess in order to attain some end that is set before us." "In geography, for example, so long as we are merely learning the bare facts of the subject, the size and contours of the different continents, the political divisions, the natural features, we are at the acquisitive stage." "But when we go on to try to find out the reasons why certain facts that we have learned should be as they are and not otherwise, we pass to the constructive stage. We are working constructively when we seek to discover why it is that great cities are so often found on the banks of rivers, why peninsulas more frequently turn southward than northward." You readily see that this constructive method of study involves the setting and solving of problems as its distinguishing feature, and that in the solution of these problems we make use of reason.

A little reflection will show that though there is a distinct difference between processes of acquisition and of construction, nevertheless the two must not be regarded as entirely separate from each other. "In acquiring new facts we must always use a little reason, while in constructive work, we cannot always rely upon having all the necessary matter ready to hand. We have frequently to stop our constructive work for a little in order to acquire some new facts that we find to be necessary. Thus we acquire a certain number of new facts while we are reasoning about things, and while we are engaged in acquiring new matter we must use our reason at least to some small extent." The two overlap, then. But there is a difference between them from the standpoint of the student, and the terms denote two fundamentally different attitudes which students take in study. The two attitudes may be illustrated by contrasting the two methods often used in studying geometry. Some students memorize the theorem and the steps in the demonstration, reciting them verbatim at class-hour.

Others do not memorize, but reason out each step to see its relation to the preceding step, and when they see it must necessarily follow, they pass on to the next and do the same. These two types of students apparently arrive at the same conclusions, but the mental operations leading up to the Q.E.D. of each are vastly different. The one student does his studying by the rote memory method, the other by the road of reasoning. The former road is usually considered the easier, and so we find it most frequently followed. To memorize a table, a definition, or a series of dates is relatively easy. One knows exactly where one is, and can keep track of one's progress and test one's success. Some people are attracted by such a task and are perfectly happy to follow this plan of study. The kind of mind that contents itself with such phonographic records, however, must be acknowledged to be a commonplace sort of affair. We recognize its limitations in ordinary life, invariably rating it lower than the mind that can reason to new conclusions and work independently. Accordingly, if we wish to possess minds of superior quality, we see that we must develop the reasoning processes.

When we examine the mental processes by which we think constructively, or, in other words, reason, we find first of all that there is recognition of a problem to be solved. When we start to reason, we do it because we find ourselves in a situation from which we must extricate ourselves. The situation may be physical, as when our automobile stops suddenly on a country road; or it may be mental, as when we are deciding what college to attend. In both cases, we recognize that we are facing a problem which must be solved.

After recognition of the problem, our next step is to start vigorous efforts to solve it. In doing this, we cast about for means; we summon all the powers at our disposal. In the case of the automobile, we call to mind other accidents and the causes of them; we remember that once the spark-plug played out, so we test this hypothesis. At another time some dust got into the carburetor, so we test this. So we go on, calling up possible causes and applying appropriate remedies until the right one is found and the engine is started. In bringing to bear upon the problem facts from our past experience, we form a series of judgments. In the case of the problem as to what college to attend, we might form these judgments: this college is nearer home; that one has a celebrated faculty; this one has good laboratories; that one is my father's alma mater. So we might go on, bringing up all the facts regarding the problem and fitting each one mentally to see how it works. Note that this utilization of ideas should not consist merely of fumbling about in a vague hope of hitting upon some solution. It must be a systematic search, guided by carefully chosen ideas. For example, "if the clock on the mantle-piece has stopped, and we have no idea how to make it go again, but mildly shake it in the hope that something will happen to set it going, we are merely fumbling. But if, on moving the clock gently so as to set the pendulum in motion, we hear it wobbling about irregularly, and at the same time observe that there is no ticking of any kind, we come to the conclusion that the pendulum has somehow or other escaped the little catch that connects it with the mechanism, we have been really thinking. From the fact that the pendulum wobbles irregularly, we infer that it has lost its proper catch. From the fact that there is no ticking, we infer the same thing, for even when there is something wrong with the clock that will prevent it from going permanently, if the pendulum is set in motion by force from without it will tick for a few seconds before it comes to rest again. The important point to observe is that there must be inference. This is always indicated by the word *therefore* or its equivalent. If you reach a conclusion without having to use or at any rate to imply a *therefore*, you may take it for granted that you have not been really thinking, but only jumping to conclusions."

This process of putting facts in the form of judgments and drawing inferences, may be likened to a court-room scene where arguments are presented to the judge. As each bit of evidence is submitted, it is subjected to the test of its applicability to the situation or to similar situations in the past. It is rigidly examined and nothing is accepted as a candidate for the solution until it is found by trial (of course, in imagination) to be pertinent to the situation.

The third stage of the reasoning process comes when some plan which has been suggested as a possible solution of the difficulty proves effective, and we make the decision; the arguments support or overthrow each other, adding to and eliminating various considerations until finally only one course appears possible. As we said before, the solution comes inevitably, as represented by the word *therefore*. Little active work on our part is necessary, for if we have gone through these other phases properly the decision will make itself. You cannot make a wrong decision if you have the facts before you and have given each the proper weight. When the solution comes, it is recognized as right, for it comes tinged with a feeling that we call belief.

Now that we have found the reasoning process to be one of problem-solving, of which the first step is to acknowledge and recognize the difficulty, the second, to call up various methods of solution, and the third, to decide on the basis of one of the solutions that comes tinged with certainty, we are ready to apply this schema to study in the hope that we may discover the causes and remedies for the reasoning difficulties of students. In view of the fact that reasoning starts out with a problem, you see at once that to make your study effective you must study in problems. Avoid an habitual attitude of mere acquisition. Do not memorize facts in the same pattern as they are handed out to you. In history, in general literature, in science, do not read facts merely as they come in the text, but seek the relations between them. Voluntarily set before yourself intellectual problems. Ask yourself, *why* is this so? In other words, in your study do not merely acquire, but also *construct.* The former makes use mostly of memory and though your memorizing be done ever so conscientiously, if it comprise the main part of your study, you fail to utilize your mind to its fullest extent.

Let us now consider the second stage of the reasoning process as found in study. At this stage the facts in the mind are brought forward for the purpose of being fitted into the present situation, and the essential thing is that you have a large number of facts at your disposal. If you are going to reason effectively about problems in history, mathematics, geography, it is absolutely indispensable that you know many facts about the subjects. One reason why you experience difficulty in reasoning about certain subjects is that you do not know enough about them. Particularly is this true in such subjects as political economy, sociology and psychology. The results of such ignorance are often demonstrated in political and social movements. Why do the masses so easily fall victims to doubtful reforms in national and municipal policies? Because they do not know enough about these matters to reason intelligently. Watch ignorant people listening to a demagogue and see what unreasonable things they accept. The speaker propounds a question and then proceeds to answer it in his own way. He makes it appear plausible, assuring his hearers it is the only way, and they agree because they do not have enough other facts at their command to refute it. They are unable, as we say, to see the situation in several aspects. The mistakes in reasoning which children make have a similar basis. The child reaches for the moon, reasoning--"Here is something bright; I can touch most bright things; therefore, I can touch this." His reasoning is fallacious because he does not have all the facts. This condition is paralleled in the class-room when students make what are shamefacedly looked back upon as miserable blunders. When one of these fiascos occurs the cause can many times be referred to the fact that the student did not have enough facts at his command. Speaking broadly, the most effective reasoning in a field can be done by one who has had the most extensive experiences in that field. If one had complete acquaintance with all facts, one would have perfect conditions for reasoning. Thus we see that effectiveness in reasoning demands an extensive array of facts. Accordingly, in your courses of study you must read with avidity. When you are given a list of readings in a course, some of which are required and some optional, read both sets, and every new fact thus secured will make you better able to reason in the field.

But good reasoning demands more than mere quantity of ideas. The ideas must conform to certain qualitative standards before they may be effectively employed in reasoning. They must arise with promptness, in an orderly manner, pertinent to the matter in hand, and they must be clear. In securing promptness of association on the part of your ideas, employ the methods described in the chapter on memory. Make many logical associations with clearness and repetition. In order to insure the rise of ideas in an orderly manner, pay attention to the manner in which you acquire them.

Remember, things will be recalled as they were impressed, so the value of your ideas in reasoning will depend upon the manner in which you make original impressions. A further characteristic of serviceable ideas is clarity. Ideas are sometimes described as "clear" in opposition to "muddy." You know what is meant by these distinctions, and you may be assured that one cause for your failures in reasoning is that your ideas are not clear. This manifests itself in inability to make clear statements and to comprehend clearly. The latter condition is easily illustrated. When you began the study of geometry you faced a multitude of new terms; we call them technical terms, such as projection, scalene, theory of limits. These had to be clearly understood before you could reason in the subject. And when, in the progress of your study, you experienced difficulty in reasoning out problems, it was very likely due to the fact that you did not master the technical terms, and as soon as you encountered the difficulties of the course, you failed because your foundation laying did not involve the acquisition of clear ideas. Examine your difficulties in reasoning subjects and if you find them traceable to vagueness of ideas, take steps to clarify them.

Ideas may be clarified in two ways: by definition and by classification. Definition is a familiar device, for you have had much to do with it in learning. The memorization of definitions is an excellent practice, not as an end in itself, but as a means to the end of effective reasoning. Throughout your study, then, pay much attention to definitions. Some you will find in your texts, but others you will have to make for yourself. In order to get practice in this, undertake the manufacture of a few definitions, using terms such as charity, benevolence, natural selection. This exercise will reveal what an exacting mental operation definition is and will prove how vague most of your thinking really is.

A large stock of definitions will help you to think rapidly. Standing as they do for a large group of experiences, definitions are a means of mental economy. For illustration of their service in reasoning, suppose you were asked to compare the serf, the peon and the American slave. If you have a clean-cut definition of each of these terms, you can readily differentiate between them, but if you cannot define them, you will hardly be able to reason concerning them.

The second means of clarifying ideas is classification. By this is meant the process of grouping similar ideas or similar points of ideas. For example, your ideas of serf, peon and slave have some points in common. Group the ideas, then, with reference to these points. Then in reasoning you can quickly place an idea in its proper group.

The third stage of the reasoning process is decision, based on belief, and it comes inevitably, provided the other two processes have been performed rightly. Accordingly, we need say little about its place in study. One caution should be pointed out in making decisions. Do not make them hastily on the basis of only one or two facts. Wait until you have canvassed all the ideas that bear importantly upon the case. The masses that listen top eagerly to the demagogue do not err merely from lack of ideas, but partly because they do not utilize all the facts at their disposal. This fault is frequently discernible in impulsive people, who notoriously make snap-judgments, which means that they decide before canvassing all the evidence. This trait marks the fundamental difference between superficial and profound thinkers. The former accept surface facts and decide immediately, while the latter refuse to decide until after canvassing many facts.

In the improvement of reasoning ability your task is mainly one of habit formation. It is necessary, first, to form the habit of stating things in the form of problems; second, to form habits by which ideas arise promptly and profusely; third, to form habits of reserving decisions until the important facts are in. These are all specific habits that must be built up if the reasoning processes of the mind are to be effective. Already you have formed some habits, if not habits of careful looking into things, then habits of hasty, heedless, impatient glancing over the surface. Apply the principles of habit formation already enunciated, and remember that with every act of reasoning you perform, you are moulding yourself into a careless reasoner or an accurate reasoner, into a clear thinker or a muddy thinker. This chapter shows that reasoning is one of the highest powers of man. It is a mark of originality and intelligence, and stamps its possessor not a copier but an originator, not a follower but a leader, not a slave, to have his thinking foisted upon him by others, but a free and independent intellect, unshackled by the bonds of ignorance and convention. The man who employs reason in acquiring knowledge, finds delights in study that are denied to a rote memorizer. When one looks at the world through glasses of reason, inquiring into the eternal *why*, then facts take on a new meaning, knowledge comes with new power, the facts of experience glow with vitality, and one's own relations with them appear in a new light.

READINGS AND EXERCISES

Readings:

Adams (1) Chapter IV.

Dearborn (2) Chapter V.

Dewey (3) Chapters III and VI.

Exercise I. Illustrate the steps of the reasoning process, by describing the way in which you studied this chapter.

Exercise 2. Try to define the following words without the assistance of a dictionary: College, university, grammatical, town-meeting.

Exercise 3. Prepare a set of maxims designed to help a student change from the "rote memory" method of study to the "reason-why" (or "problem") method.

CHAPTER X

EXPRESSION AS AN AID IN STUDY

In our discussion of the nervous basis underlying study we observed that nerve pathways are affected not only by what enters over the sensory pathways, but also by what flows out over the motor pathways. As the nerve currents travel out from the motor centres in the brain to the muscles, they leave traces which modify future thoughts and actions. This being so, it is easy to see that what we give out is fully as important as what we take in; in other words, our *expressions* are just as important as our *impressions*. By expressions we mean the motor consequences of our thoughts, and in study they usually take the form of speech and writing of a kind to be specified later.

The far-reaching effects of motor expressions are too infrequently emphasized, but psychology forces us to give them prime consideration. We are first apprised of their importance when we study the nervous system, and find that every incoming sensory message pushes on and on until it finds a motor pathway over which it may travel and produce movement. This is inevitable. The very structure and arrangement of the neurones is such that we are obliged to make some movement in response to objects affecting our sense organs. The extent of movement may vary from the wide-spread tremors that occur when we are frightened by a thunderstorm to the merest flicker of an eye-lash. But whatever be its extent, movement invariably occurs when we are stimulated by some object. This has been demonstrated in startling ways in the psychological laboratory, where even so simple a thing as a piece of figured wall-paper has been shown to produce measurable bodily disturbances. Ordinarily we do not notice these because they are so slight, sometimes being merely twitches of deep-seated muscles or slight enlargements or contractions of arteries which are very responsive to nerve currents. But no matter how large or how small, we may be sure that movements always occur on the excitation of a sense organ. This led us to assert in an earlier chapter that the function of the nervous system is to convert incoming sensory currents into outgoing motor currents.

So ingrained is this tendency toward movement that we do not need even a sensory cue to start it off; an idea will do as well. In other words, the nervous current need not start at a sense organ, but may start in the brain and still produce movement. This fact is embodied in the law of ideo-motor action (distinguished from sensory-motor action), "every idea in the mind tends to express itself in movement." This motor character of ideas is manifested in a most thorough-going way and renders our muscular system a faithful mirror of our thoughts. We have in the psychological laboratory delicate apparatus which enables us to measure many of these slight movements. For example, we fasten a recording device to the top of a person's head, so that his slightest movements will be recorded, then we ask him while standing perfectly still to think of an object at his right side. After several moments the record shows that he involuntarily leans in the direction of the object about which he is thinking. We find further illustration of this law when we examine people as they read, for they involuntarily accompany the reading with movements of speech, measurable in the muscles of the throat, the tongue and the lips. These facts, and many others, constitute good evidence for the statement that ideas seek expression in movement.

The ethical consequences of this are so momentous that we must remark upon them in passing. We now see the force of the biblical statement, "Not that which entereth into the mouth defileth the man; but that which proceedeth out of the mouth, this defileth the man." Think what it means to one's character that every thought harbored in the mind is bound to come out. It may not manifest itself at once in overt action, but it affects the motor pathways and either weakens or strengthens connections so that when the opportunity comes, some act will be furthered or hindered. In view of the proneness to permit base thoughts to enter the mind, human beings might sometimes fear even to think. A more optimistic idea, however, is that noble thoughts lead to noble acts. Therefore, keep in your mind the kind of thoughts that you wish to see actualized in your character and the appropriate acts will follow of their own accord.

But it is with the significance of expressions in study that we are at present concerned, and here we find them of supreme importance. We ordinarily regard learning as a process of taking things into the mind, and regard expression as a thing apart from acquisition of knowledge. We shall find in this discussion, however, that there is no such sharp demarcation between acquiring knowledge and expressing knowledge, but that the two are intimately bound together, expressions being properly a part of wise and economical learning.

When we survey the modes of expression that may be used in study, we find them to be of several kinds. Speech is one. This is the form of expression for which the class-recitation is provided. If you wish to grow as a student, utilize the recitation period and welcome every chance to recite orally, for things about which you recite in class are more effectively learned. Talking about a subject under all circumstances will help you learn. When studying subjects like political economy, sociology or psychology, seize every opportunity to talk over the questions involved. Hold frequent conferences with your instructor; voice your difficulties freely, and the very effort to state them will help to clarify them. It is a good plan for two students in the same course to come together and talk over the problems; the debates thus stimulated and the questions aroused by mental interaction are very helpful in impressing facts more vividly upon the mind.

Writing is a form of expression and is one thing that gives value to note-taking and examinations. Its value is further recognized by the requirements of themes and term-papers. These are all mediums by which you may develop yourself, and they merit your earnest cooperation.

Another medium of expression that students may profitably employ is drawing. This is especially valuable in such subjects as geology, physiology and botany. Students in botany are compelled to do much drawing of the plant-forms which they study, and this is a wise requirement, for it makes them observe more carefully, report more faithfully and recall with greater ease. You may secure the same advantages by employing the graphic method in other studies. For example, when reading in a geology text-book about the stratification of the earth in a certain region, draw the parts described and label them according to the description. You will be surprised to see how clear the description becomes and how easily it is later recalled.

Let us examine the effects of the expressive movements of speech, writing and the like, and see the mechanism by which they facilitate the study process. We may describe their effects in two ways: neurologically and psychologically. As may be expected from our preliminary study of the nervous system, we see their first effects upon the motor pathways leading out to the muscles. Each passage of the nerve current from brain to muscle leaves traces so that the resulting act is performed with greater ease upon each repetition. This fact has already been emphasized by the warning, Guard the avenues of expression.

Especially is it important at the first performance of an act, because this determines the path of later performances. In such studies as piano-playing, vocalizing and pronunciation of foreign words, see that your first performance is absolutely right, then as the expressive movements are repeated, they will be more firmly ingrained because of the deepening of the motor pathways.

The next effect of acts of expression is to be found in the modifications made in the sensory areas of the brain. You will recall that every movement of a muscle produces nervous currents which go back to the brain and register there in the form of kinaesthetic sensations. To demonstrate kinaesthetic sensations, close your eyes and move your index finger up and down. You can feel the muscles contracting and the tendons moving back and forth, even into the back of the hand. These sensations ordinarily escape our attention, but they occupy a prominent place in the control of our actions. For example, when ascending familiar stairs in the dark, they notify us when we have reached the top. We are still further impressed with their importance when we are deprived of them; when we try to walk upon a foot or a leg that has gone "to sleep"; that is, when the kinaesthetic nerves are temporarily paralyzed we find it difficult to walk. But besides being used to control muscular actions, they may be used in study, for they may be made the source of impressions, and impressions, as we learned in the chapter on memory, are a prime requisite for learning. Each expression becomes, then, through its kinaesthetic results, the source of new impressions, when, for example, you pronounce the German word, *anwenden*, with the English word "to employ," in addition to the impressions made through the ear, you make impressions through the muscles of speech (kinaesthetic impressions), and these kinaesthetic impressions enter into the body of your knowledge and later may serve as the means by which the word may be revived. When you write the word, you make kinaesthetic impressions which may later serve as forms of revival. So the movements of expression produce sensory material that may serve as tentacles by means of which you can later reach back into your memory and recall facts.

We shall now consider another service of expressions which, though little regarded, nevertheless is of much moment. When we make expressive movements, much nervous energy is generated; much more than during passive impression. Energy is sent back to the brain over the kinaesthetic nerve cells, and the greater the extent of the movement, the greater is the amount of new energy sent to the brain. It pours into the brain and diffuses itself especially throughout the association areas. Here it excites regions which could not be excited by a more limited amount of energy. This means, in psychical terms, that new ideas are being aroused. The obvious inference from this fact is that you may, by starting movements of expression, actually summon to your assistance added powers of mind. For example, when you are called upon to recite in class, your mind seems to be a complete blank--in a state of "deadlock." You may break this "deadlock" and start brain-action by some kind of movement. It may be only to clear your throat, to ejaculate "well," or to squirm about in the seat, but whatever form the movement takes, it will usually be effective in creating the desired nervous energy, and after the inertia is once overcome the mental stream will flow freely. The unconscious application of this device is seen when a man is called on suddenly to make a speech for which he has not prepared. He usually starts out by telling a story, thus liberating nervous energy to pour back into the brain and start thinking processes. With increasing vehemence of expression, the ideas come more and more freely, and the result is a speech which surpasses the expectations of the speaker himself. The gesticulations of many speakers have this same function, being frequently of great service in arousing more nervous energy, which goes back to the brain and arouses more ideas.

The device of stimulating ideas by expressive movements may be utilized in theme- or letter-writing. It is generally recognized that the difficult thing in such writing is to get a start, and the too common practice is to sit listlessly gazing into space waiting for "inspiration." This is usually a futile procedure. The better way is to begin to write anything about the topic in hand. What you write may have little merit, either of substance or form. Nevertheless, if you persist in keeping up the activity of writing, making more and more movements, you will find that the ideas will begin to come in greater profusion until they come so fast you can hardly write them down.

Having tried to picture the neural effect of expression, we may now translate them into psychological terms, asking what service the expressions render to the conscious side of our study. First of all, we note that the expressions help to make the acts and ideas in study habitual. We find ourselves, with each expression, better able to perform such acts as the pronunciation of foreign words. Second, they furnish new impressions through the kinaesthetic sense, thus being a source of sense-impression. Third, they give rise to a greater number of ideas and link them up with the idea dominant at the moment. There is a further psychological effect of expression in the clarification of ideas. It is a well-attested fact that when we attempt to explain a thing to someone else, it becomes clearer in our own minds. You can demonstrate this for yourself by attempting to explain to someone an intricate conception such as the nebular hypothesis. The effort involved in making the explanation makes the fact more vivid to you. The habit of thus utilizing your knowledge in conversation is an excellent one to acquire. Indeed, expression is the only objective test of knowledge and we cannot say that we really know until we can express our knowledge. Expression is thus the great clarification agency and the test of knowledge. Before leaving this discussion, it might be well to remark upon one phase of expression that is sometimes a source of difficulty. This is the embarrassment incident to some forms of expression, notably oral. Many people are deterred from utilizing this form of expression because of shyness and embarrassment in the presence of others. If you have this difficulty in such excess that it hinders you from free expression, resolve at once to overcome it. Begin at the very outset of your academic career to form habits of disregarding your impulses to act in frightened manner. Take a course in public speaking. The practice thus secured will be a great aid in developing habits of fearless and free oral expression.

This discussion has shown that expression is a powerful aid in learning, and is a most important feature of mental life. Cultivate your powers of expression, for your college education should consist not only in the development of habits of impression, but also in the development of habits of expression. Grasp eagerly every opportunity for the development of skill in clear and forceful expression. Devote assiduous attention to themes and all written work, and make serious efforts to speak well. Remember you are forming habits that will persist throughout your life. Emphasize, therefore, at every step, methods of expression, for it is this phase of learning in which you will find greatest growth.

EXERCISE

Exercise I. Give an example from your own experience, showing how expression (a) stimulates ideas, (b) clarifies ideas.

CHAPTER XI

HOW TO BECOME INTERESTED IN A SUBJECT

"I can't get interested in Mediaeval History." This illustrates a kind of complaint frequently made by college students. It is our purpose in this chapter to show the fallacy of this; to prove that interest may be developed in an "uninteresting" subject; and to show how.

In order to lay a firm foundation for our psychologizing, let us examine into the nature of interest and see what it really is. It has been defined as: "the recognition of a thing which has been vitally connected with experience before--a thing recognized as old"; "impulse to attend"; "interest naturally arouses tendencies to act"; "the root idea of the term seems to be that of being engaged, engrossed, or entirely taken up with some activity because of its recognized worth"; "interest marks the annihilation of the distance between the person and the materials and results of his action; it is the sign of their organic union."

In addition to the characteristics just mentioned should be noted the pleasurableness that usually attends any activity in which we are "interested." A growing feeling of pleasure is the sign which notifies us that we are growing interested in a subject. And it is such an aid in the performance of work that we should seek earnestly to acquire it in connection with any work we have to do.

The persons who make the complaint at the head of this chapter notice that they take interest easily in certain things: a Jack London story, a dish of ice cream, a foot-ball game. And they take interest in them so spontaneously and effortlessly that they think these interests must be born within them.

When we examine carefully the interests of man, and trace their sources, we see that the above view is fallacious. We acquire most of our interests in the course of our experience. Professor James asserts: "An adult man's interests are almost every one of them intensely artificial; they have been slowly built up. The objects of professional interest are most of them in their original nature, repulsive; but by their connection with such natively exciting objects as one's personal fortune, one's social responsibilities and especially by the force of inveterate habit, they grow to be the only things for which in middle life a man profoundly cares."

Since interests are largely products of experience, then, it follows that if we wish to have an interest in a given subject, we must consciously and purposefully develop it. There is wide choice open to us. We may develop interest in early Victorian literature, prize-fight promoting, social theory, lignitic rocks, history of Siam, the collection of scarabs, mediaeval history.

We should not be deceived by the glibness of the above statements into assuming that the development of interest is an easy matter. It requires adherence to certain definite psychological laws which we may call the laws of interest. The first may be stated as follows: _In order to develop interest in a subject, secure information about it_. The force of this law will be apparent as soon as we analyze one of our already-developed interests. Let us take one that is quite common--the interest which a typical young girl takes in a movie star. Her interest in him comes largely from what she has been able to learn about him; the names of the productions in which he has appeared, his age, the color of his automobile, his favorite novel. Her interest may be said actually to consist, at least in part, of these facts. The astute press agent knows the force of this law, and at well-timed intervals he lets slip through bits of information about the star, which fan the interest of the fair devotee to a still whiter heat.

The relation of information to interest is still further illustrated by the case of the typical university professor or scientist. He is interested in certain objects of research--infusoria, electrons, plant ecology,--because he knows so much about them. His interest may be said to *consist* partly of the body of knowledge that he possesses. He was not always interested in the specific, obscure field, but by saturating himself in facts about it, he has developed an interest in it amounting to passionate absorption, which manifests itself in "absent-mindedness" of such profundity as to make him often an object of wonder and ridicule.

Let us demonstrate the application of the law again showing how interest may be developed in a specific college subject. Let us choose one that is generally regarded as so "difficult" and "abstract" that not many people are interested in it--philology, the study of language as a science. Let us imagine that we are trying to interest a student of law in this. As a first step we shall select some legal term and show what philology can tell about it. A term frequently encountered in law is indenture--a certain form of contract. Philological researches have uncovered an interesting history regarding this word. It seems that in olden days when two persons made an agreement they wrote it on two pieces of paper, then notched the edges so that when placed together, the notches on the edge of one paper would just match those of the other. This protected both parties against substitution of a fraudulent contract at time of fulfillment.

Still earlier in man's development, before he could write, it was customary to record such agreements by breaking a stick in two pieces and leaving the jagged ends to be fitted together at time of fulfillment. Sometimes a bone was used this way. Because its critical feature was the saw-toothed edge, this kind of contract was called indenture (derived from the root *dent*--tooth, the same one from which we derive our word dentist).

The formal, legal-looking document which we today call an indenture gives us no hint of its humble origin, but the word when analyzed by the technique of philology tells the whole story, and throws much light upon the legal practices of our forbears. Having discovered one such valuable fact in philology, the student of law may be led to investigate the science still further and find many more. As a result still he will become interested in philology.

By this illustration we have demonstrated the first psychological law of interest, and also its corollary which is: _State the new in terms of the old_. For we not only gave our lawyer new information culled from philological sources; we also introduced our fact in terms of an old fact which was already "interesting" to the lawyer. This is recognized as such an important principle in education that it has become embodied in a maxim: Proceed from the known to the unknown.

A classic example of good educational practice in this connection is the way in which Francis W. Parker, a progressive educator of a former generation, taught geography. When he desired to show how water running over hard rocky soil produced a Niagara, he took his class down to the creek behind the school house, built a dam and allowed the water to flow over it. When he wished to show how water flowing over soft ground resulted in a deltoid Nile, he took the class to a low, flat portion of the creek bed and pointed out the effect. The creek bed constituted an old familiar element in the children's experience. Niagara and the Nile described in terms of it were intelligible.

Naturally in modern educational practice it is not always possible to have miniature waterfalls and river bottoms at hand, still it is possible to follow this principle. When, in studying Mediaeval History, you read a description of the guilds, do not regard them as distant, cold, inert institutions devoid of significance in your life. Rather, think of them in terms of things you already know: modern Labor Unions, technical schools, in so far as the comparison holds good. Then trace their industrial descendants down to the present time. By thus thinking about the guilds, hitherto distant and uninteresting, you will begin to see them suffused with meaning, alight with significance, a real part of yourself. In short, you will have achieved interest.

There is still another psychological law of interest: _In order to develop interest in a subject, exert activity toward it_. We see the force of this law when we observe a man in the process of developing an interest in golf. At the start he may have no interest in it whatever; he may even deride it. Yielding to the importunities of his friends, however, he takes his stick in hand and samples the game. Then he begins to relent; admits that perhaps there may be something interesting about the game after all. As he practises with greater frequency he begins to develop a warmer and still warmer interest until finally he thinks of little else; neglecting social and professional obligations and boring his friends *ad nauseum* with recitals of golfing incidents. The methods by which the new-fledged golfer develops an interest in golf will apply with equal effectiveness in the case of a student. In trying to become interested in Mediaeval History, keep actively engaged in it. Read book after book dealing with the subject. Apply it to your studies in Political Economy, English, and American History. Choose sub-topics in Mediaeval History as the subjects for themes in English composition courses. Try to help some other student in the class. Take part in class discussions and talk informally with the instructor outside of the classroom. Use your ingenuity to devise methods of keeping active toward the subject. Presently you will discover that the subject no longer appears cold and forbidding; but that it glows warm with virility; that it has become interesting.

It will readily be noticed that the two laws of interest here set forth are closely interrelated. One can hardly seek information about a subject without exerting activity toward it; conversely, one cannot maintain activity on behalf of a subject without at the same time acquiring information about it. These two easily-remembered and easily-applied rules of study will go far toward solving some of the most trying conditions of student life. Memorize them, apply them, and you will find yourself in possession of a power which will stay with you long after you quit college walls; one which you may apply with profit in many different situations of life.

We have shown in this chapter the fallacy of the assumption that a student cannot become genuinely interested in a subject which at first seems uninteresting.

We have shown that he may develop interest in any subject if he but employs the proper psychological methods. That he must obey the two-fold law--secure information about the subject (stating the new in terms of the old) and exert activity toward it. That when he has thus lighted the flame of interest, he will find his entire intellectual life illuminated, glowing with purpose, resplendent with success.

In concluding this discussion we should note the wide difference between the quality of study which is done with interest and that done without it. Under the latter condition the student is a slave, a drudge; under the former, a god, a creator. Touched by the galvanic spark he sees new significance in every page, in every line. As his vision enlarges, he perceives new relations between his study and his future aims, indeed, between his study and the progress of the universe. And he goes to his educational tasks not as a prisoner weighted down by ball and chain, but as an eager prospector infatuated by the lust for gold. Encouraged by the continual stores of new things he uncovers, intoxicated by the ozone of mental activity, he delves continually deeper until finally he emerges rich with knowledge and full of power--the intellectual power that signifies mastery over a subject.

READINGS AND EXERCISES

Readings: James (8) Chapters X and XI. Dewey (3)

Exercise I. Show how your interest in some subject, for example, the game of foot-ball, has grown in proportion to the number of facts you have discovered about it and the activity you have exerted toward it.

Exercise 2. Choose some subject in which you are not at present interested. Make the statement:--"I am determined to develop an interest in--. I will take the following specific steps toward this end."

CHAPTER XII

THE PLATEAU OF DESPOND

In our investigation of the psychology of study we have so far directed our attention chiefly toward the subjective side of the question, seeking to discover the *contents* of mind during study. We shall now take an objective view of study, examining not the contents of mind nor methods of study, but the objective results of study. In doing this, we choose certain units of measurement, the number of minutes required for learning a given amount or the amount learned in a stated period of time. We may do this for the learning of any material, whether it be Greek verbs or typewriting. All that is necessary is to decide upon some method by which progress can be noted and expressed in numerical units. This, you will observe, constitutes a statistical approach to the processes of study, such as is employed in science; and just as the statistical method has been useful in science, so it may be of value in education, and by means of statistical investigations of learning we may hope to discover some of the factors operative in good learning.

Progress in learning is best observable when we represent our measurements graphically, when they take the form of a curve, variously called "the curve of efficiency," "practice curve," "learning curve." We shall take a sample curve for the basis of our discussion, showing the progress of a beginner in the Russian language for sixty-five days (indicated in the figure by horizontal divisions). The student studied industriously for thirty minutes each day and then translated as rapidly as possible for fifteen minutes, the number of words translated being represented by the vertical spaces on the chart. Thus, on the tenth day, twenty-five words were translated, on the twentieth day, forty-five words.

[Illustration (graph): STUDY OF RUSSIAN]

In making an analysis of this typical curve, we note immediately an exceeding irregularity. At one time there is extraordinary improvement, but a later measurement registers pronounced loss. This irregularity is very common in learning. Some days we do a great amount of work and do it well, but perhaps the very next day shows marked diminution in our work.

The second characteristic we note is that there is extremely rapid progress at the beginning, the curve slanting up quite sharply. This is common in learning, and may be accounted for in several ways. In the first place, the easiest things come first. For example, when you are beginning the study of German, you are given mostly monosyllabic words to learn. These are easily remembered, hence progress is rapid. A second reason is that at the beginning there are many different respects in which progress can be made. For example, the beginner in German must learn nouns, case endings, declension of adjectives, days of the week; in short, a vast number of new things all at once. At a later period however, the number of new things to be learned is much smaller and improvement cannot be so rapid. A third reason why learning proceeds more rapidly at first is that the interest is greater at this time. You have doubtless many times experienced this fact, and you know that when a thing has the interest of novelty you work harder upon it.

If you will examine the learning curve closely, you will note that after the initial spurt, there is a slowing up. The curve at this point resembles a plateau and indicates cessation of progress if not retrogression. This period of no progress is regarded as a characteristic of the learning curve and is a time of great discouragement to the conscientious student, so distressing that we may designate it "the plateau of despond." Most people describe it as a time when they feel unable to learn more about a subject; the mind seems to be sated; new ideas cannot be assimilated, and old ones seem to be forgotten. The plateau may extend for a long or a short time, depending upon the nature of the subject-matter and the length of time over which the learning extends. In the case of professional training, it may extend over a year or more. In the case of growing children in school, it sometimes happens that an entire year elapses during which the learning of an apparently bright student is retarded. In a course of study in high school or college, it may come on about the third week and extend a month or more. Something akin to the plateau may come in the course of a day, when we realize that our efficiency is greatly diminished and we seem, for an hour or more, to make no progress.

Inasmuch as the plateau is such a common occurrence in human activity, we should analyze it and see what factors operate to influence it. It is interesting to note that the plateau generally occurs just before an abrupt rise in efficiency. This is significant, for it may mean that the plateau is necessary in learning, especially just before reaching the really advanced stages of proficiency. Accordingly, when you are experiencing a plateau in the mastery of some accomplishment, you may perhaps derive some comfort from the prospect of an approaching rise in efficiency. On the theory that it is a necessary part of learning, it has been regarded as a resting place. We are so constituted by nature that we cannot run on indefinitely; nature sometimes must call a halt. Consequently, the plateau may be a warning that we cannot learn more for the present and that the proper remedy is to refrain for a little while from further efforts in that line. We have possible justification for this interpretation when we reflect that a vacation does us much good, and though we begin it feeling stale, we end it feeling much fresher and more efficient.

But to stop work temporarily is not the only way to meet a plateau, and fatigue or ennui is probably not the sole or most compelling explanation. It may be that we should not regard the objective results as the true measure of learning; perhaps learning is going on even though the results are not apparent. We discovered something in the nature of unconscious learning in our discussion of memory, and it may be that a period of little objective progress marks a period of active unconscious learning.

Another meaning which the plateau may have is simply to mark places of greater difficulty. As already remarked, the early period is a stage of comparative ease, but as the work becomes more difficult, progress is slower. It is also quite likely that the plateau may indicate that some of the factors operative at the start are operative no longer. Thus, although the learning was rapid at the beginning because the material learned at that time was easy, the plateau may come because the things to be learned have become difficult. Or, whereas the beginning was attacked with considerable interest, the plateau may mean that the interest is dying down, and that less effort is being exerted.

If these theories are the true explanation of the plateau, we see that it is not to be regarded as a time of reduction in learning, to be contemplated with despair. The appropriate attitude may be one of resignation, with the determination to make it as slightly disturbing as possible. But though the reasons just described may have something to do with the production of the plateau, as yet we have no evidence that the plateau cannot be dispensed with. It is practically certain that the plateau is not caused entirely by necessity for rest or unconscious learning. It frequently is due, we must regretfully admit, to poor early preparation. If at the beginning of a period of learning an insecure foundation is laid, it cannot be expected to support the burden of more difficult subject-matter.

We have enumerated a number of the explanations that have been advanced to account for the plateau, and have seen that it may have several causes, among which are necessity for rest, increased difficulty of subject-matter, loss of interest and insufficient preparation. In trying to eliminate the plateau, our remedy should be adapted to the cause. In recognition of the fact that learning proceeds irregularly, we see that it is rational to expect the amount of effort to be exerted throughout a period of learning, to vary. It will vary partly with the difficulty of subject-matter and partly with fluctuations in bodily and mental efficiency which are bound to occur from day to day. Since this irregularity is bound to occur, you may well make your effort vary from one extreme to the other. At times, perhaps your most profitable move may be to take a complete vacation. The vacation might cover several weeks, a week-end, or if the plateau is merely a low period in the day's work, then ten minutes may suffice for a vacation. As an adjunct to such rest periods, some form of recreation should usually be planned, for the essential thing is to permit the mind to rest from the tiresome activity.

If your plateau represents greater difficulty of subject-matter and loss of interest, your duty is plainly to work harder. In exerting more effort, make some changes in your methods of study. For example, if you have been accustomed to study a certain subject by silent reading, begin to read your lessons aloud. Change your method of taking notes, or change the hour of day in which you prepare your lesson. In short, try any of the methods described in this book, and use your own ingenuity, and the change in method may overcome the plateau.

If a plateau is due to our last-mentioned cause, insufficient preparation, the remedy must be drastic. To make new resolutions and to put forth additional effort is not enough; you must go back and relay the foundation. Make a thorough review of the work which you covered slightingly, making sure that every step is clear. This process was described in an earlier chapter as the clarification of ideas and is absolutely essential in building up a structure of knowledge that will stand. Indeed, as you take various courses you will find that your study will be much improved by periodical reviews. The benefits cannot all be enumerated here, but we may reasonably claim that a review will be very likely to remove a plateau, and used with the other remedies herein suggested, will help you to rid yourself of one of the most discouraging features of student life.

READING AND EXERCISE

Reading: Swift (20) Chapter IV.

Exercise I. Describe one or more plateaus that you have observed in your own experience. What do you regard as the causes?

CHAPTER XIII

MENTAL SECOND-WIND

Did you ever engage in any exhausting physical work for a long period of time? If so, you probably remember that as you proceeded, you became more and more fatigued, finally reaching a point when it seemed that you could not endure the strain another minute. You had just decided to give up, when suddenly the fatigue seemed to diminish and new energy seemed to come from some source. This curious thing, which happens frequently in athletic activities, is known as second-wind, and is described, by those who have experienced it, as a time of increased power, when the work is done with greater ease and effectiveness and with a freshness and vigor in great contrast to the staleness that preceded it. It is as though one "tapped a level of new energy," revealing hidden stores of unexpected power. And it is commonly reported that with persistence in pushing one's self farther and farther, a third and fourth wind may be uncovered, each one leading to greater heights of achievement.

This phenomenon occurs not alone on the physical plane; it is discernible in mental exertion as well. True, we seldom experience it because we are mentally lazy and have the habit of stopping our work at the first signs of fatigue. Did we persist, however, disregarding fatigue and ennui, we should find ourselves tapping vast reserves of mental power and accomplishing mental feats of astonishing brilliancy.

The occasional occurrence of the phenomenon of second-wind gives ground for the statement that we possess more energy than we ordinarily use. There are several lines of evidence for this statement.

One is to be found in the energizing effects of emotional excitement. Under the impetus of anger, a man shows far greater strength than he ordinarily uses. Similarly, a mother manifests the strength of a tigress when her young is endangered. A second line of evidence is furnished by the effect of stimulants. Alcohol brings to the fore surprising reserves of physical and psychic energy. Lastly, we have innumerable instances of accession of strength under the stimulus of an idea. Under the domination of an all-absorbing idea, one performs feats of extraordinary strength, utilizing stores of energy otherwise out of reach. We have only to read of the heroic achievements of little Joan of Arc for an example of such manifestation of reserve power.

When we examine this accession of energy we find it to be describable in several ways--physiologically, neurologically and psychologically. The physiological effects consist in a heightening of the bodily functions in general. The muscles become more ready to act, the circulation is accelerated, the breathing more rapid. Curious things take place in various glands throughout the body. One, the adrenal gland, has been the object of special study and has been shown, upon the arousal of these reserves of energy, to produce a secretion of the utmost importance in providing for sudden emergencies. This little gland is located above the kidney, and is aroused to intense activity at times, pouring out into the blood a fluid that goes all over the body. Some of its effects are to furnish the blood with chemicals that act as fuel to the muscles, assisting them to contract more vigorously, to make the lungs more active in introducing oxygen into the system, to make the heart more active in distributing the blood throughout the body. Such glandular activity is an important physiological condition of these higher levels of energy. In neurological terms, the increase in energy consists in the flow of more nervous energy into the brain, particularly into those areas where it is needed for certain kinds of controlled thought and action. An abundance of nervous energy is very advantageous, for, as has been intimated in a former chapter, nervous energy is diffused and spread over all the pathways that are easily permeable to its distribution. This results in the use of considerable areas of brain surface, and knits up many associations, so that one idea calls up many other ideas. This leads us to recognize the psychological conditions of increased energy, which are, first, the presence of more ideas, second, the more facile flow of ideas; the whole accompanied by a state of marked pleasurableness. Pleasure is a notable effect of increased energy. When work progresses rapidly and satisfactorily, it is accomplished with great zest and a feeling almost akin to exaltation. These conditions describe to some degree the conditions when we are doing efficient work.

Since we are endowed with the energy requisite for such efficient work, the obvious question is, why do we not more frequently use it? The answer is to be found in the fact that we have formed the habit of giving up before we create conditions of high efficiency. You will note that the conditions require long-continued exertion and resolute persistence. This is difficult, and we indulgently succumb to the first symptoms of fatigue, before we have more than scratched the surface of our real potentialities.

Because of the prominent place occupied by fatigue in thus being responsible for our diminished output, we shall briefly consider its place in study. Everyone who has studied will agree that fatigue is an almost invariable attendant of continuous mental exertion. We shall lay down the proposition at the start, however, that the awareness of fatigue is not the same as the objective fatigue in the organs of the body. Fatigue should be regarded as a twofold thing--a state of mind, designated its subjective aspect, and a condition of various parts of the body, designated its objective aspect. The former is observable by introspection, the latter by analysis of bodily secretions and by measurement of the diminution of work, entirely without reference to the way the mind regards the work. Fatigue subjectively, or fatigue as we *feel* it, is not at all the same as fatigue as manifested in the body. If we were to make two curves, the one showing the advancement of the *feeling* of fatigue, and the other showing the advancement of impotence on the part of the bodily processes, the two curves would not at all coincide. Stated another way, fatigue is a complex thing, a product of ideas, feelings and sensations, and sometimes the ideas overbalance the sensations and we think we are more tired then we are objectively. It is this fact that accounts for our too rapid giving up when we are engaged in hard work.

A psychological analysis of the subjective side of fatigue will make its true nature more apparent. Probably the first thing we find in the mind when fatigued is a large mass of sensations. They are referred to various parts of the body, mostly the part where muscular activity has been most violent and prolonged. Not all of the sensations, however, are intense enough to be localizable, some being so vague that we merely say we are "tired all over." These vague sensations are often overlooked; nevertheless, as will be shown later, they may be exceedingly important.

But sensations are not the only contents of the mind at time of fatigue. Feelings are present also, usually of a very unpleasant kind. They are related partly to the sensations mentioned above, which are essentially painful, and they are feelings of boredom and ennui. We have yet to examine the ideas in mind and their behavior at time of fatigue. They come sluggishly, associations being made slowly and inaccurately, and we make many mistakes. But constriction of ideas is not the sole effect of fatigue. At such a time there are usually other ideas in the mind not relevant to the fatiguing task of the moment, and exceedingly distracting. Often they are so insistent in forcing themselves upon our attention that we throw up the work without further effort. It is practically certain that much of our fatigue is due, not to real weariness and inability to work, but to the presence of ideas that appear so attractive in contrast with the work in hand that we say we are tired of the latter. What we really mean is that we would rather do something else. These obtruding ideas are often introduced into our minds by other people who tell us that we have worked long enough and ought to come and play, and though we may not have felt tired up to this point, still the suggestion is so strong that we immediately begin to feel tired. Various social situations can arouse the same suggestion. For example, as the clock nears quitting time, we feel that we ought to be tired, so we allow ourselves to think we are.

Let us now examine the bodily conditions to see what fatigue is objectively. "Physiologically it has been demonstrated that fatigue is accompanied by three sorts of changes. First, poisons accumulate in the blood and affect the action of the nervous system, as has been shown by direct analysis. Mosso ... selected two dogs as nearly alike as possible. One he kept tied all day; the other, he exercised until by night it was thoroughly tired. Then he transfused the blood of the tired animal into the veins of the rested one and produced in him all the signs of fatigue that were shown by the other. There can be no doubt that the waste products of the body accumulate in the blood and interfere with the action of the nerve cells and muscles. It is probable that these accumulations come as a result of mental as well as of physical work.

"A second change in fatigue has been found in the cell body of the neurone. Hodge showed that the size of the nucleus of the cell in the spinal cord of a bee diminished nearly 75 per cent, as a result of the day's activity, and that the nucleus became much less solid. A third change that has been demonstrated as a result of muscular work is the accumulation of waste products in the muscle tissue. Fatigued muscles contain considerable percentages of these products. That they are important factors in the fatigue process has been shown by washing them from a fatigued muscle. As a result the muscle gains new capacity for work. The experiments are performed on the muscles of a frog that have been cut from the body and fatigued by electrical stimulation. When they will no longer respond, their sensitivity may be renewed by washing them in dilute alcohol or in a weak salt solution that will dissolve the products of fatigue. It is probable that these products stimulate the sense-organs in the muscles and thus give some of the sensations of fatigue. Of these physical effects of fatigue, the accumulation of waste products in the blood and the effects upon the nerve cells are probably common both to mental and physical fatigue. The effect upon the muscles plays a part in mental fatigue only so far as all mental work involves some muscular activity."

By this time you must be convinced that the subject of fatigue is exceedingly complicated; that its effects are manifested differently in mind and body. In relieving fatigue the first step to be taken is to rest properly. Man cannot work incessantly; he must rest sometimes, and it is just as important to know how to rest efficiently as to know how to work efficiently. By this is not meant that one should rest as soon as fatigue begins to be felt. Quite the reverse. Keep on working all the harder if you wish the second-wind to appear. Perhaps two hours will exhaust your first supply of energy and will leave you greatly fatigued. Do not give up at this time, however. Push yourself farther in order to uncover the second layer of energy. Before entering upon this, however, it will be possible to secure some advantage by resting for about fifteen minutes. Do not rest longer than this, or you may lose the momentum already secured and your two hours will have gone for naught. If one indulges in too long a rest, the energy seems to run down and more effort is required to work it up again than was originally expended. It is also important to observe the proper mental conditions during rest. Do not spend the fifteen minutes in getting interested in some other object; for that will leave distracting ideas in the mind which will persist when you resume work. Make the rest a time of physical and mental relief. Move cramped muscles, rest your eyes and let your thoughts idly wander; then come back to work in ten or fifteen minutes and you will be amazed at the refreshed feeling with which you do your work and at the accession of new energy that will come to you. Keep on at this new plane and your work will take on all the attributes of the second-wind level of efficiency.

Besides planning intelligent rests, you may also adjust yourself to fatigue by arranging your daily program so as to do your hardest work when you are fresh, and your easiest when your efficiency is low. In other words, you are a human dynamo, and should adjust yourself to the different loads you carry. When carrying a heavy load, employ your best energies, but when carrying only a light load, exert a proportionate amount of energy. Every student has tasks of a routine nature which do not require a high degree of energy, such as copying material. Plan to perform such work when your stock of energy is lowest.

One of the best ways to insure the attainment of a higher plane of mental efficiency is to assume an attitude of interestedness. This is an emotional state and we have seen that emotion calls forth great energy.

A final aid in promoting increase of energy is that gained through stimulating ideas. Other things being equal, the student who is animated by a stimulating idea works more diligently and effectively than one without. The idea may be a lofty professional ideal; it may be a desire to please one's family, a sense of duty, or a wish to excel. Whatever it is, an idea may stimulate to extraordinary achievements. Adopt some compelling aim if you have none. A vocational aim often serves as a powerful incentive throughout one's student life. An idea may operate for even more transient purposes; it may make one oblivious to present discomfort to a remarkable degree. This is accomplished through the aid of suggestion. When feelings of fatigue approach, you may ward them off by resolutely suggesting to yourself that you are feeling fresh.

Above all, the will is effective in lifting one to higher levels of efficiency. It is notorious that a single effort of the will, "such as saying 'no' to some habitual temptation or performing some courageous act, will launch a man on a higher level of energy for days and weeks, will give him a new range of power. 'In the act of uncorking the whiskey bottle which I had brought home to get drunk upon,' said a man to me, 'I suddenly found myself running out into the garden, where I smashed it on the ground. I felt so happy and uplifted after this act, that for two months I wasn't tempted to touch a drop.'" But the results of exertions of the will are not usually so immediate, and you may accept it as a fact that in raising yourself to a higher level of energy you cannot do it by a single effort. Continuous effort is required until the higher levels of energy have *formed the habit* of responding when work is to be done. In laying the burden upon Nature's mechanism of habit, you see you are again face to face with the proposition laid down at the beginning of the book--that education consists in the process of forming habits of mind. The particular habit most important to cultivate in connection with the production of second-wind is the habit of resisting fatigue. Form the habit of persisting in spite of apparent obstacles and limitations. Though they seem almost unsurmountable, they are really only superficial. Buried deep within you are stores of energy that you yourself are unaware of. They will assist you in accomplishing feats far greater than you think yourself capable of. Draw upon these resources and you will find yourself gradually living and working upon a higher plane of efficiency, improving the quality of your work, increasing the quantity of your work and enhancing your enjoyment in work.

READINGS AND EXERCISE

Readings: James (9) Seashore (14) Chapter III. Swift (20) Chapter V.

Exercise I. Describe conditions you have observed at time of second-wind in connection with prolonged (a) physical exertion, (b) intellectual exertion.

CHAPTER XIV

EXAMINATIONS

One of the most vexatious periods of student life is examination time. This is almost universally a time of great distress, giving rise in extreme cases to conditions of nervous collapse. The reason for this is not far to seek, for upon the results of examinations frequently depend momentous consequences, such as valuable appointments, diplomas, degrees and other important events in the life of a student. In view of the importance of examinations, then, it is natural that they be regarded with considerable fear and trepidation, and it is important that we devise what rules we can for meeting their exactious demands with greatest ease and effectiveness.

Examinations serve several purposes, the foremost of which is to inform the examiner regarding the amount of knowledge possessed by the student. In discovering this, two methods may be employed; first, to test whether or not the student knows certain things, plainly a reproductive exercise; second, to see how well the student can apply his knowledge. But this is not the only function of an examination. It also shows the student how much he knows or does not know. Again the examination often serves as an incentive to harder work on the part of the student, for if one knows there will be an examination in a subject, one usually studies with greater zeal than when an examination is not expected. Lastly, an examination may help the student to link up facts in new ways, and to see them in new relationships. In this aspect, you readily see that examinations constitute a valuable device in learning.

But students are not very patient in philosophizing about the purpose of examinations, declaring that if examinations are a necessary part of the educational process, they wish some advice that will enable them to pass examinations easily and with credit to themselves. So we shall turn our attention to the practical problems of passing examinations.

Our first duty in giving advice is to call attention to the necessity for faithful work throughout the course of study. Some students seem to think that they can slight their work throughout a course, and by vigorous cramming at the end make up for slighted work and pass the examination. This is an extremely dangerous attitude to take. It might work with certain kinds of subject-matter, a certain type of student-mind and a certain kind of examiner, but as a general practice it is a most treacherous method of passing a course. The greatest objection from a psychological standpoint is that we have reason to believe that learning thus concentrated is not so permanently effective as that extended over a long period of time. For instance, a German course extending over a year has much to commend it over a course with the same number of recitation-hours crowded into two months. We already discussed the reasons for this in Chapter VI, when we showed the beneficial results coming from the distribution of impressions over a period of time.

Against cramming it may further be urged that the hasty impression of a mass of new material is not likely to be lasting; particularly is this true when the cramming is made specifically for a certain examination. As we saw in the chapter on memory, the intention to remember affects the firmness of retention, and if the cramming is done merely with reference to the examination, the facts learned may be forgotten and never be available for future use. So we may lay it down as a rule that feverish exertions at the end of a course cannot replace conscientious work throughout the course. In spite of these objections, however, we must admit that cramming has some value, if it does not take the form of new acquisition of facts, but consists more of a manipulation of facts already learned. As a method of review, it has an eminently proper place and may well be regarded as indispensable. Some students, it is true, assert that they derive little benefit from a pre-examination review, but one is inclined to question their methods. We have already found that learning is characteristically aided by reviews, and that recall is facilitated by recency of impression. Reviewing just before examination serves the memory by providing repetition and recency, which, as we learned in the chapter on memory, are conditions for favorable impression.

A further value of cramming is that by means of such a summarizing review one is able to see facts in a greater number of relations than before. It too often happens that when facts are taken up in a course they come in a more or less detached form, but at the conclusion of the course a review will show the facts in perspective and will disclose many new relations between them.

Another advantage of cramming is that at such a time, one usually works at a high plane of efficiency; the task of reviewing in a few hours the work of an entire course is so huge that the attention is closely concentrated, impressions are made vividly, and the entire mentality is tuned up so that facts are well impressed, coordinated and retained. These advantages are not all present in the more leisurely learning of a course, so we see that cramming may be regarded as a useful device in learning.

We must not forget that many of the advantages secured by cramming are dependent upon the methods pursued. There are good methods and poor methods of cramming. One of the most reprehensible of the latter is to get into a flurry and scramble madly through a mass of facts without regard to their relation to each other. This method is characterized by breathless haste and an anxious fear lest something be missed or forgotten. Perhaps its most serious evil is its formlessness and lack of plan. In other words the facts should not be seized upon singly but should be regarded in the light of their different relations with each other. Suppose, for example, you are reviewing for an examination in mediaeval history. The important events may be studied according to countries, studying one country at a time, but that is not sufficient; the events occurring during one period in one country should be correlated with those occurring in another country at the same time. Likewise the movements in the field of science and discovery should be correlated with movements in the fields of literature, religion and political control. Tabulate the events in chronological order and compare the different series of events with each other. In this way the facts will be seen in new relations and will be more firmly impressed so that you can use them in answering a great variety of questions.

Having made preparation of the subject-matter of the examination, the next step is to prepare yourself physically for the trying ordeal, for it is well known that the mind acts more ably under physically healthful conditions. Go to the examination-room with your body rested after a good night's sleep. Eat sparingly before the examination, for mental processes are likely to be clogged if too heavy food is taken.

Having reached the examination-room, there are a number of considerations that are requisite for success. Some of the advice here given may seem to be superfluous but if you had ever corrected examination papers you would see the need of it all. Let your first step consist of a preliminary survey of the examination questions; read them all over slowly and thoughtfully in order to discover the extent of the task set before you. A striking thing is accomplished by this preliminary reading of the questions. It seems as though during the examination period the knowledge relating to the different questions assembles itself, and while you are focusing your attention upon the answer to one question, the answers to the other questions are formulating themselves in your mind. It is a semi-conscious operation, akin to the "unconscious learning" discussed in the chapter on memory. In order to take advantage of it, it is necessary to have the questions in mind as soon as possible; then it will be found that relevant associations will form and will come to the surface when you reach the particular questions.

During the examination when some of these associations come into consciousness ahead of time, it is often wise to digress from the question in hand long enough to jot them down. By all means preserve them, for if you do not write them down they may leave you and be lost. Sometimes very brilliant ideas come in flashes, and inasmuch as they are so fleeting, it is wise to grasp them and fix them while they are fresh.

In writing the examination, be sure you read every question carefully. Each question has a definite point; look for it, and do not start answering until you are sure you have found it. Discover the implications of each question; canvass its possible interpretations, and if it is at all ambiguous seek light from the instructor if he is willing to make any further comment.

It is well to have scratch paper handy and make outlines for your answers to long questions. It is a good plan, also, when dealing with long questions, to watch the time carefully, for there is danger that you will spend too much time upon some question to the detriment of others equally important, though shorter.

One error which students often commit in taking examinations is to waste time in dreaming. As they come upon a difficult question they sit back and wait for the answer to come to them. This is the wrong plan. The secret of freedom of ideas lies in activity. Therefore, at such times, keep active, so that the associative processes will operate freely. Stimulate brain activity by the method suggested in Chapter X, namely, by means of muscular activity. Instead of idly waiting for flashes of inspiration, begin to write. You may not be able to write directly upon the point at issue, but you can write something about it, and as you begin to explore and to express your meagre fund of knowledge, one idea will call up another and soon the correct answer will appear.

After you have prepared yourself to the extent of your ability, you should maintain toward the examination an attitude of confidence. Believe firmly that you will pass the examination. Make strong suggestions to yourself, affirming positively that you have the requisite amount of information and the ability to express it coherently and forcefully. Fortified by the consciousness of faithful application throughout the work of a course, reinforced by a thorough, well-planned review, and with a firm conviction in the strength of your own powers, you may approach your examinations with comparative ease and with good chances of passing them creditably.

READINGS AND EXERCISE

Readings:

Adams (1) Chapter X.

Dearborn (2) Chapter II.

Exercise I. Make a schedule of your examinations for the next examination week. Show exactly what preparatory steps you will take

(a) before coming to the examination room, (6) after entering it.

CHAPTER XV

BODILY CONDITIONS FOR EFFECTIVE STUDY

It is a truism to say that mental ability is affected by bodily conditions. A common complaint of students is that they cannot study because of a headache, or they fail in class because of loss of sleep. So patent is the interrelation between bodily condition and study that we cannot consider our discussion of study problems complete without recognition of the topic. We shall group our discussions about three of the most important physical activities, eating, sleeping and exercising. These make up the greater part of our daily activities and if they are properly regulated our study is likely to be effective.

FOOD.--It is generally agreed that the main function of food is to repair the tissues of the body. Other effects are present, such as pleasure and sociability, but its chief benefit is reparative, so we may well regard the subject from a strictly utilitarian standpoint and inquire how we may produce the highest efficiency from our eating. Some of the important questions about eating are, how much to eat, what kind of food to eat, when to eat, what are the most favorable conditions for eating?

The quantity of food to be taken varies with the demands of the individual appetite and the individual powers of absorption. In general, one who is engaged in physical labor needs more, because of increased appetite and increased waste of tissues. So a farm-hand needs more food than a college student, whose work is mostly indoors and sedentary. Much has been said recently about the ills of overeating. One of the most enthusiastic defenders of a decreased diet is Mr. Horace Fletcher, who, by the practice of protracted mastication, "contrives to satisfy the appetite while taking an exceptionally small amount of food. Salivary digestion is favored and the mechanical subdivision of the food is carried to an extreme point. Remarkably complete digestion and absorption follow. By faithfully pursuing this system Mr. Fletcher has vastly bettered his general health, and is a rare example of muscular and mental power for a man above sixty years of age. He is a vigorous pedestrian and mountain-climber and holds surprising records for endurance tests in the gymnasium.

"The chief gain observed in his case, as in others which are more or less parallel, is the acquiring of immunity to fatigue, both muscular and central. It is not claimed that the sparing diet confers great strength for momentary efforts--'explosive strength,' as the term goes--but that moderate muscular contractions may be repeated many times with far less discomfort than before. The inference appears to be that the subject who eats more than is best has in his circulation and his tissues by-products which act like the muscular waste which is normally responsible for fatigue. According to this conception he is never really fresh for his task, but is obliged to start with a handicap. When he reduces his diet the cells and fluids of his body free themselves of these by-products and he realizes a capacity quite unguessed in the past.

"The same assumption explains the fact mentioned by Mr. Fletcher, that the hours of sleep can be reduced decidedly when the diet is cut down. It would seem as though a part of our sleep might often be due to avoidable auto-intoxication. If one can shorten his nightly sleep without feeling the worse for it this is an important gain."

But the amount of food is probably not so important as the kind. Foods containing much starch, as potatoes and rice, may ordinarily be taken in greater quantities than foods containing much protein, such as meats and nuts. So our problem is not so much concerned with quantity as with the choice of kinds of food. Probably the most favorable distribution of foods for students is a predominance of fruits, coarse cereals, starch and sugar and less prominence to meats. Do not begin the day's study on a breakfast of cakes. They are a heavy tax upon the digestive powers and their nutritive value is low. The mid-day meal is also a crucial factor in determining the efficiency of afternoon study, and many students almost completely incapacitate themselves for afternoon work by a too-heavy noon meal. Frequently an afternoon course is rendered quite valueless because the student drowses through the lecture soddened by a heavy lunch. One way of overcoming this difficulty is by dispensing with the mid-day meal;

another way is to drink a small amount of coffee, which frequently keeps people awake; but these devices are not to be universally recommended.

The heavy meal of a student may well come at evening. It should consist of a varied assortment of foods with some liquids, preferably clear soup, milk and water. Meat also forms a substantial part of this meal, though ordinarily it should not be taken more than once a day. Much is heard nowadays about the dangers of excessive meat-eating and the objections are well-founded in the case of brain-workers. The undesirable effects are "an unprofitable spurring of the metabolism--more particularly objectionable in warm weather--and the menace of auto-intoxication." Too much protein, found in meat, lays a burden upon the liver and kidneys and when the burden is too great, wastes, which cannot be taken care of, gather and poison the blood, giving rise to that feeling of being "tired all over" which is so inimical to mental and physical exertion. When meat is eaten, care should be taken to choose right kinds. "Some kinds of meat are well known to occasion indigestion. Pork and veal are particularly feared. While we may not know the reason why these foods so often disagree with people, it seems probable that texture is an important consideration. In both these meats the fibre is fine, and fat is intimately mingled with the lean. A close blending of fat with nitrogenous matter appears to give a fabric which is hard to digest. The same principle is illustrated by fat-soaked fried foods. Under the cover of the fat, thorough-going bacterial decomposition of the proteins may be accomplished with the final release of highly poisonous products. Attacks of acute indigestion resulting from this cause are much like the so-called ptomaine poisoning."

Much of the benefit of meat may be secured from other foods. Fat, for example, may be obtained from milk and butter freed from the objectionable qualities of the meat-fibre. In this connection it is important to call attention to the use of fried fat. Avoid fat that is mixed with starch particles in such foods as fried potatoes and pie-crust.

The conditions during meals should always be as pleasant as possible. This refers both to physical surroundings and mental condition. "The processes occurring in the alimentary canal are greatly subject to influences radiating from the brain. It is especially striking that both the movements of the stomach and the secretion of the gastric juice may be inhibited as a result of disturbing circumstances. Intestinal movements may be modified in similar fashion."

"Cannon has collected various instances of the suspension of digestion in consequence of disagreeable experiences, and it would be easy for almost anyone to add to his list. He tells us, for example, of the case of a woman whose stomach was emptied under the direction of a specialist in order to ascertain the degree of digestion undergone by a prescribed breakfast. The dinner of the night before was recovered and was found almost unaltered. Inquiry led to the fact that the woman had passed a night of intense agitation as the result of misconduct on the part of her husband. People who are seasick some hours after a meal vomit undigested food. Apprehension of being sick has probably inhibited the gastric activities.

"Just as a single occasion of painful emotion may lead to a passing digestive disturbance, so continued mental depression, worry, or grief may permanently impair the working of the (alimentary) tract and undermine the vigor and capacity of the sufferer. Homesickness is not to be regarded lightly as a cause of malnutrition. Companionship is a powerful promoter of assimilation. The attractive serving of food, a pleasant room, and good ventilation are of high importance. The lack of these, so commonly faced by the lonely student or the young man making a start in a strange city, may be to some extent counteracted by the cultivation of optimism and the mental discipline which makes it possible to detach one's self from sordid surroundings."

Almost as important as eating is drinking, for liquids constitute the "largest item in the income" of the body. Free drinking is recommended by physiologists, the beneficial results being, "the avoidance of constipation, and the promotion of the elimination of dissolved waste by the kidneys and possibly the liver." In regard to the use of water with meals, a point upon which emphatic cautions were formerly offered, recent experiments have failed to show any bad effects from this, and the advice is now given to drink "all the water that one chooses with meals." Caution should be observed, however, about introducing hot and cold liquids into the stomach in quick succession.

Other liquids have been much discussed by dietitians, especially tea and coffee. "These beverages owe what limited food value they have to the cream and sugar usually mixed with them. They give pleasure by their aroma, but they are given a peculiar position among articles of diet by the presence in them of the compound caffein, which is distinctly a drug. It is a stimulant to the heart, the kidneys, and the central nervous system."

"Individual susceptibility to the action of caffein varies greatly. Where one person notices little or no reaction after a cup of coffee, another is exhilarated to a marked degree and hours later may find himself lying sleepless with tense or trembling muscles, a dry, burning skin, and a mind feverishly active. Often it is found that a more protracted disturbance follows the taking of coffee with cream than is caused by black coffee.

"It is too much to claim that the use of tea and coffee is altogether to be condemned. Many people, nevertheless, are better without them. For all who find themselves strongly stimulated it is the part of wisdom to limit the enjoyment of these decoctions to real emergencies when uncommon demands are made upon the endurance and when for a time hygienic considerations have to be ignored. If young people will postpone the formation of the habit they will have one more resource when the pressure of mature life becomes severe."

Before concluding this discussion a word might be added concerning the relation between fasting and mental activity. Prolonged abstinence from food frequently results in highly sharpened intellectual powers. Numerous examples of this are found in the literature of history and biography; many actors, speakers and singers habitually fast before public performances. There are some disadvantages to fasting, especially loss of weight and weakness, but when done under the direction of a physician, fasting has been known to produce very beneficial effects. It is mentioned here because it has such marked effects in speeding up the mental processes and clearing the mind; and the well-nourished student may find the practice a source of mental strength during times of stress such as examinations.

SLEEP.--"About one-third of an average human life is passed in the familiar and yet mysterious state which we call sleep. From one point of view this seems a large inroad upon the period in which our consciousness has its exercise; a subtraction of twenty-five years from the life of one who lives to be seventy-five. Yet we know that the efficiency and comfort of the individual demand the surrender of all this precious time. It has often been said that sleep is a more imperative necessity than food, and the claim seems to be well founded." It is quite likely that some students indulge in too much sleep. This may sometimes be due to laziness, but frequently it is due to actual intoxication, from an excess of food which results in the presence of poisonous "narcotizing substances absorbed from the burdened intestine". This theory is rendered tenable by the fact that when the diet is reduced the hours of sleep may be reduced. If one is in good health, it seems right to expect that one should be able to arise gladly and briskly upon awaking. By all means do not indulge yourself in long periods of lying in bed after a good night's rest. If we examine the physical and physiological conditions of sleep we shall better understand its hygiene. Sleep is a state in which the tissues of the body which have been used up may be restored. Of course some restoration of broken-down tissue takes place as soon as it begins to wear out, but so long as the body keeps working, the one process can never quite compensate for the other, so there must be a periodic cessation of activity so that the energies of the body may be devoted to restoration. Viewing sleep as a time when broken-down bodily cells are restored, we see that we tax the energies of the body less if we go to sleep each day before the cells are entirely depleted. That is the significance of the old teaching that sleep before midnight is more efficacious than sleep after midnight. It is not that there is any mystic virtue in the hours before twelve, but that in the early part of the evening the cells are not so nearly exhausted as they are later in the evening, and it is much easier to repair them in the partially exhausted stage than it is in the completely exhausted stage. For this reason, a mid-day nap is often effective, or a short nap after the evening dinner. By thus catching the cells at an early stage of their exhaustion, they can be restored with comparative ease, and more energy will be available for use during the remainder of the working hours.

A problem that may occasionally trouble a student is sleeplessness and we may properly consider here some of the ways of avoiding it. One prime cause of sleeplessness is external disturbance. The disturbance may be visual. Although it is ordinarily thought that if the eyes are closed, no visual disturbances can be sensed, nevertheless, as a matter of fact the eye-lids are not wholly opaque. Sight may be obtained through them, as you may prove by closing your eyes and moving your fingers before them. The lids transmit light to the retina and it is quite likely that you are frequently awakened by a beam of light falling upon your closed eye-lids. For this reason, one who is inclined to be wakeful should shut out from the bed-room all avenues whereby light may enter as a distraction.

The temperature sense is also a source of distraction in sleep, and it is a common experience to be awakened by extreme cold. The ears, too, may be the source of disturbance in sleep; for even though we are asleep, the tympanic membrane is always exposed to vibrations of air. In fact, stimuli are continually playing upon the sense-organs and are arousing nervous currents which try to break over the boundaries of sleep and impress themselves upon the brain.

For this reason, one who wishes to have untroubled sleep should remove all possible distractions.

But apart from external distractions, wakefulness may still be caused by distractions from within. Troublesome ideas may be present and persist in keeping one awake. This means that brain activity has been started and needs suppression. Various devices have been suggested. One is to eat something very light, just enough to draw the surplus blood, which excites the brain, away from the brain to the digestive tract. This advice should be taken with caution, however, for eating just before retiring may use up in digestion much of the energy needed in repairing the body, and may leave one greatly fatigued in the morning.

One way to relieve the mind of mental distractions is to fill it with non-worrisome, restful thoughts. Read something light, a restful essay or a non-exciting story, or poetry. Another device is to bathe the head in cold water so as to relieve congestion of blood in the brain. A tepid or warm bath is said to have a similar effect.

Dreams constitute one source of annoyance to many, and while they are not necessarily to be avoided, still they may disturb the night's rest. We may avoid them in some measure by creating conditions free from sensory distractions, for many of our dreams are direct reflections of sensations we are experiencing at the moment. A dream with an arctic setting may be the result of becoming uncovered on a cold night. To use an illustration from Ellis: "A man dreams that he enlists in the army, goes to the front, and is shot. He is awakened by the slamming of a door. It seems probable that the enlistment and the march to the field are theories to account for the report which really caused the whole train of thought, though it seemed to be its latest item." Such dreams may be partially eliminated by care in arranging conditions so that there will be few distractions. Especially should they be guarded against in the later hours of the sleep, for we do not sleep so soundly after the first two hours as we do before, and stimuli can more easily impress themselves and affect the brain.

Before leaving the subject of sleep, we should note the benefit to be derived from regularity in sleep. All Nature seems to move rhythmically and sleep is no exception. Insomnia may be treated by means of habituating one's self to get sleepy at a certain time, and there is no question that the rising process may be made easier if one forms the habit of arising at the same time every morning. To rhythmize this important function is a long step towards the efficient life.

EXERCISE.--Brain workers do not ordinarily get all the exercise they should. Particularly is this true of some conscientious students who feel they must not take any time from their study. But this denotes a false conception of mental action. The human organism needs exercise. Man is not a disembodied spirit; he must pay attention to the claims of the body. Indeed it will be found that time spent in exercise will result in a higher grade of mental work. This is recognized by colleges and universities by the requirement of gymnasium work, and the opportunity should be welcomed by the student. Inasmuch as institutions generally give instruction in this subject, we need not go specifically into the matter of exercises. Perhaps the only caution that need be urged is that against the excessive participation in such exhausting games as foot-ball. It is seriously to be questioned whether the strenuous grilling that a foot-ball player must undergo does not actually impair his ability to concentrate upon his studies.

If you undertake a course of exercise, by all means have it regular. Little is gained by sporadic exercising. Adopt the principle of regularity and rhythmize this important phase of bodily activity as well as all other phases.

In concluding our discussion of physical hygiene for the student, we cannot stress too much the value of relaxation. The life of a student is a trying one. It exercises chiefly the higher brain centres and keeps the organism keyed up to a high pitch. These centres become fatigued easily and ought to be rested occasionally. Therefore, the student should relax at intervals, and engage in something remote from study. To forget books for an entire week-end is often wisdom; to have a hobby or an avocation is also wise. A student must not forget that he is something more than an intellectual being. He is a physical organism and a social being, and the well-rounded life demands that all phases receive expression. We grant that it is wrong to exalt the physical and stunt the mental, but it is also wrong to develop the intellectual and neglect the physical. We must recognize with Browning that,

all good things Are ours, nor soul helps flesh more, now, than flesh helps soul.

READINGS AND EXERCISE

Readings:

Patrick (14) Chapters I, II and VII. Stiles (18) and (19).

Swift (20) Chapter X.

Exercise 1. With the help of a book on dietetics prepare an ideal day's bill of fare for a student.

SUGGESTIONS FOR FURTHER READING

Besides the standard texts in general and educational psychology, the following books bear with especial intimacy upon the topics treated in this book:

1. Adams, John, Making the Most of One's Mind, New York: George H. Doran Co., 1915.

2. Dearborn, George V., How to Learn Easily, Boston: Little, Brown & Co., 1918.

3. Dewey, John, How we Think, Boston: D.C. Heath & Co., 1910.

4. Dewey, John, Interest and Effort in Education, Boston: Houghton, Mifflin Co., 1913.

5. Fulton, Maurice (ed.), College Life, Its Conditions and Problems, The Macmillan Co., 1915.

6. Hall-Quest, Alfred L., Supervised Study, New York: The Macmillan Co., 1916.

7. Herrick, C. Judson, An Introduction to Neurology, Philadelphia: W.B. Saunders Co., 1915.

8. James, William, Talks to Teachers on Psychology, and to Students on Some of Life's Ideals, New York. 1899.

9. James, William, The Energies of Men, New York: Moffatt, Yard & Co., 1917.

10. Kerfoot, John B., How to Read, Boston: Houghton, Mifflin & Co., 1916.

11. Lockwood, Francis (comp.), The Freshman and His College, Boston: D.C. Heath & Co., 1913.

12. Lowe, John Adams, Books and Libraries, Boston: The Boston Book Co., 1917.

13. McMurry, Frank M., How to Study, Boston: Houghton, Mifflin & Co., 1909.

14. Patrick, George T. W., The Psychology of Relaxation, Boston: Houghton, Mifflin & Co., 1916.

15. Sandwick, Richard L., How to Study and What to Study, Boston: D.C. Heath & Co., 1915.

16. Seashore, Carl E., Psychology in Daily Life, New York: D. Appleton & Co., 1918.

17. Seward, S., Note-taking, Boston: Allyn & Bacon, 1910.

18. Stiles, Percy G., Nutritional Physiology Philadelphia: W. B. Saunders Co., 1912.

19. Stiles, Percy G., The Nervous System and Its Conservation, Philadelphia: W.B. Saunders Co., 1914.

20. Swift, Edgar J., Psychology and the Day's Work, New York: C. Scribner's Sons, 1919.

21. Watt, Henry J., The Economy and Training of Memory, New York: Longmans, Green & Co., 1909.

22. Whipple, Guy M., How to Study Effectively, Bloomington, Ill.: Public School Publishing Co., 1916.

INDEX

Synapse

Theme writing

"Unconscious" learning see memory

Will

Writing a form of expression

---

do practically ANYTHING with public domain eBooks. Redistribution is subject to the trademark license, especially commercial redistribution.

1.C. The Project Gutenberg Literary Archive Foundation ("the Foundation" or PGLAF), owns a compilation copyright in the collection of Project Gutenberg-tm electronic works. Nearly all the individual works in the collection are in the public domain in the United States. If an individual work is in the public domain in the United States and you are located in the United States, we do not claim a right to prevent you from copying, distributing, performing, displaying or creating derivative works based on the work as long as all references to Project Gutenberg are removed. Of course, we hope that you will support the Project Gutenberg-tm mission of promoting free access to electronic works by freely sharing Project Gutenberg-tm works in compliance with the terms of this agreement for keeping the Project Gutenberg-tm name associated with the work. You can easily comply with the terms of this agreement by keeping this work in the same format with its attached full Project Gutenberg-tm License when you share it without charge with others.

1.D. The copyright laws of the place where you are located also govern what you can do with this work. Copyright laws in most countries are in a constant state of change. If you are outside the United States, check the laws of your country in addition to the terms of this agreement before downloading, copying, displaying, performing, distributing or creating derivative works based on this work or any other Project Gutenberg-tm work. The Foundation makes no representations concerning the copyright status of any work in any country outside the United States.

1.E. Unless you have removed all references to Project Gutenberg:

1.E.1. The following sentence, with active links to, or other immediate access to, the full Project Gutenberg-tm License must appear prominently whenever any copy of a Project Gutenberg-tm work (any work on which the phrase "Project Gutenberg" appears, or with which the phrase "Project Gutenberg" is associated) is accessed, displayed, performed, viewed, copied or distributed:

This eBook is for the use of anyone anywhere at no cost and with almost no restrictions whatsoever. You may copy it, give it away or re-use it under the terms of the Project Gutenberg License included with this eBook or online at www.gutenberg.net

1.E.2. If an individual Project Gutenberg-tm electronic work is derived from the public domain (does not contain a notice indicating that it is posted with permission of the copyright holder), the work can be copied and distributed to anyone in the United States without paying any fees or charges. If you are redistributing or providing access to a work with the phrase "Project Gutenberg" associated with or appearing on the work, you must comply either with the requirements of paragraphs 1.E.1 through 1.E.7 or obtain permission for the use of the work and the Project Gutenberg-tm trademark as set forth in paragraphs 1.E.8 or 1.E.9.

1.E.3. If an individual Project Gutenberg-tm electronic work is posted with the permission of the copyright holder, your use and distribution must comply with both paragraphs 1.E.1 through 1.E.7 and any additional terms imposed by the copyright holder. Additional terms will be linked to the Project Gutenberg-tm License for all works posted with the permission of the copyright holder found at the beginning of this work.

1.E.4. Do not unlink or detach or remove the full Project Gutenberg-tm License terms from this work, or any files containing a part of this work or any other work associated with Project Gutenberg-tm.

1.E.5. Do not copy, display, perform, distribute or redistribute this electronic work, or any part of this electronic work, without prominently displaying the sentence set forth in paragraph 1.E.1 with active links or immediate access to the full terms of the Project Gutenberg-tm License.

1.E.6. You may convert to and distribute this work in any binary, compressed, marked up, nonproprietary or proprietary form, including any word processing or hypertext form. However, if you provide access to or distribute copies of a Project Gutenberg-tm work in a format other than "Plain Vanilla ASCII" or other format used in the official version posted on the official Project Gutenberg-tm web site (www.gutenberg.net), you must, at no additional cost, fee or expense to the user, provide a copy, a means of exporting a copy, or a means of obtaining a copy upon request, of the work in its original "Plain Vanilla ASCII" or other form. Any alternate format must include the full Project Gutenberg-tm License as specified in paragraph 1.E.1.

1.E.7. Do not charge a fee for access to, viewing, displaying, performing, copying or distributing any Project Gutenberg-tm works unless you comply with paragraph 1.E.8 or 1.E.9.

1.E.8. You may charge a reasonable fee for copies of or providing access to or distributing Project Gutenberg-tm electronic works provided that

- You pay a royalty fee of 20% of the gross profits you derive from the use of Project Gutenberg-tm works calculated using the method you already use to calculate your applicable taxes. The fee is owed to the owner of the Project Gutenberg-tm trademark, but he has agreed to donate royalties under this paragraph to the Project Gutenberg Literary Archive Foundation. Royalty payments must be paid within 60 days following each date on which you prepare (or are legally required to prepare) your periodic tax returns. Royalty payments should be clearly marked as such and sent to the Project Gutenberg Literary Archive Foundation at the address specified in Section 4, "Information about donations to the Project Gutenberg Literary Archive Foundation."

- You provide a full refund of any money paid by a user who notifies you in writing (or by e-mail) within 30 days of receipt that s/he does not agree to the terms of the full Project Gutenberg-tm License. You must require such a user to return or destroy all copies of the works possessed in a physical medium and discontinue all use of and all access to other copies of Project Gutenberg-tm works.

- You provide, in accordance with paragraph 1.F.3, a full refund of any money paid for a work or a replacement copy, if a defect in the electronic work is discovered and reported to you within 90 days of receipt of the work.

- You comply with all other terms of this agreement for free distribution of Project Gutenberg-tm works.

1.E.9. If you wish to charge a fee or distribute a Project Gutenberg-tm electronic work or group of works on different terms than are set forth in this agreement, you must obtain permission in writing from both the Project Gutenberg Literary Archive Foundation and Michael Hart, the owner of the Project Gutenberg-tm trademark. Contact the Foundation as set forth in Section 3 below.

1.F.

1.F.1. Project Gutenberg volunteers and employees expend considerable effort to identify, do copyright research on, transcribe and proofread public domain works in creating the Project Gutenberg-tm collection. Despite these efforts, Project Gutenberg-tm electronic works, and the medium on which they may be stored, may contain "Defects," such as, but not limited to, incomplete, inaccurate or corrupt data, transcription errors, a copyright or other intellectual property infringement, a defective or damaged disk or other medium, a computer virus, or computer codes that damage or cannot be read by your equipment.

1.F.2. LIMITED WARRANTY, DISCLAIMER OF DAMAGES - Except for the "Right of Replacement or Refund" described in paragraph 1.F.3, the Project Gutenberg Literary Archive Foundation, the owner of the Project Gutenberg-tm trademark, and any other party distributing a Project Gutenberg-tm electronic work under this agreement, disclaim all liability to you for damages, costs and expenses, including legal fees. YOU AGREE THAT YOU HAVE NO REMEDIES FOR NEGLIGENCE, STRICT LIABILITY, BREACH OF WARRANTY OR BREACH OF CONTRACT EXCEPT THOSE PROVIDED IN PARAGRAPH F3. YOU AGREE THAT THE FOUNDATION, THE TRADEMARK OWNER, AND ANY DISTRIBUTOR UNDER THIS AGREEMENT WILL NOT BE LIABLE TO YOU FOR ACTUAL, DIRECT, INDIRECT, CONSEQUENTIAL, PUNITIVE OR INCIDENTAL DAMAGES EVEN IF YOU GIVE NOTICE OF THE POSSIBILITY OF SUCH DAMAGE.

1.F.3. LIMITED RIGHT OF REPLACEMENT OR REFUND - If you discover a defect in this electronic work within 90 days of receiving it, you can receive a refund of the money (if any) you paid for it by sending a written explanation to the person you received the work from. If you received the work on a physical medium, you must return the medium with your written explanation. The person or entity that provided you with the defective work may elect to provide a replacement copy in lieu of a refund. If you received the work electronically, the person or entity providing it to you may choose to give you a second opportunity to receive the work electronically in lieu of a refund. If the second copy is also defective, you may demand a refund in writing without further opportunities to fix the problem.

1.F.4. Except for the limited right of replacement or refund set forth in paragraph 1.F.3, this work is provided to you 'AS-IS," WITH NO OTHER WARRANTIES OF ANY KIND, EXPRESS OR IMPLIED, INCLUDING BUT NOT LIMITED TO WARRANTIES OF MERCHANTIBILITY OR FITNESS FOR ANY PURPOSE.

1.F.5. Some states do not allow disclaimers of certain implied warranties or the exclusion or limitation of certain types of damages. If any disclaimer or limitation set forth in this agreement violates the law of the state applicable to this agreement, the agreement shall be interpreted to make the maximum disclaimer or limitation permitted by the applicable state law. The invalidity or unenforceability of any provision of this agreement shall not void the remaining provisions.

1.F.6. **INDEMNITY**

- You agree to indemnify and hold the Foundation, the trademark owner, any agent or employee of the Foundation, anyone providing copies of Project Gutenberg-tm electronic works in accordance with this agreement, and any volunteers associated with the production, promotion and distribution of Project Gutenberg-tm electronic works, harmless from all liability, costs and expenses, including legal fees, that arise directly or indirectly from any of the following which you do or cause to occur: (a) distribution of this or any Project Gutenberg-tm work, (b) alteration, modification, or additions or deletions to any Project Gutenberg-tm work, and (c) any Defect you cause.

Section 2. Information about the Mission of Project Gutenberg-tm

Project Gutenberg-tm is synonymous with the free distribution of electronic works in formats readable by the widest variety of computers including obsolete, old, middle-aged and new computers. It exists because of the efforts of hundreds of volunteers and donations from people in all walks of life.

Volunteers and financial support to provide volunteers with the assistance they need, is critical to reaching Project Gutenberg-tm's goals and ensuring that the Project Gutenberg-tm collection will remain freely available for generations to come. In 2001, the Project Gutenberg Literary Archive Foundation was created to provide a secure and permanent future for Project Gutenberg-tm and future generations. To learn more about the Project Gutenberg Literary Archive Foundation and how your efforts and donations can help, see Sections 3 and 4 and the Foundation web page at http://www.pglaf.org.

Section 3. Information about the Project Gutenberg Literary Archive Foundation

The Project Gutenberg Literary Archive Foundation is a non profit 501(c)(3) educational corporation organized under the laws of the state of Mississippi and granted tax exempt status by the Internal Revenue Service. The Foundation's EIN or federal tax identification number is 64-6221541. Its 501(c)(3) letter is posted at http://pglaf.org/fundraising. Contributions to the Project Gutenberg Literary Archive Foundation are tax deductible to the full extent permitted by U.S. federal laws and your state's laws.

The Foundation's principal office is located at 4557 Melan Dr. S. Fairbanks, AK, 99712., but its volunteers and employees are scattered throughout numerous locations. Its business office is located at 809 North 1500 West, Salt Lake City, UT 84116, (801) 596-1887, email business@pglaf.org. Email contact links and up to date contact information can be found at the Foundation's web site and official page at http://pglaf.org

For additional contact information: Dr. Gregory B. Newby Chief Executive and Director gbnewby@pglaf.org

Section 4. Information about Donations to the Project Gutenberg
Literary Archive Foundation

Project Gutenberg-tm depends upon and cannot survive without wide
spread public support and donations to carry out its mission of
increasing the number of public domain and licensed works that can
be freely distributed in machine readable form accessible by the widest
array of equipment including outdated equipment. Many small
donations ($1 to $5,000) are particularly important to maintaining tax
exempt status with the IRS.

The Foundation is committed to complying with the laws regulating
charities and charitable donations in all 50 states of the United States.
Compliance requirements are not uniform and it takes a considerable
effort, much paperwork and many fees to meet and keep up with these
requirements. We do not solicit donations in locations where we have
not received written confirmation of compliance. To SEND
DONATIONS or determine the status of compliance for any particular
state visit http://pglaf.org

While we cannot and do not solicit contributions from states where we
have not met the solicitation requirements, we know of no prohibition
against accepting unsolicited donations from donors in such states
who approach us with offers to donate.

International donations are gratefully accepted, but we cannot make
any statements concerning tax treatment of donations received from
outside the United States. U.S. laws alone swamp our small staff.

Please check the Project Gutenberg Web pages for current donation
methods and addresses. Donations are accepted in a number of other
ways including including checks, online payments and credit card
donations. To donate, please visit: http://pglaf.org/donate

Section 5. General Information About Project Gutenberg-tm electronic
works.

Professor Michael S. Hart is the originator of the Project Gutenberg-tm
concept of a library of electronic works that could be freely shared with

anyone. For thirty years, he produced and distributed Project Gutenberg-tm eBooks with only a loose network of volunteer support.

Project Gutenberg-tm eBooks are often created from several printed editions, all of which are confirmed as Public Domain in the U.S. unless a copyright notice is included. Thus, we do not necessarily keep eBooks in compliance with any particular paper edition.

Each eBook is in a subdirectory of the same number as the eBook's eBook number, often in several formats including plain vanilla ASCII, compressed (zipped), HTML and others.

Corrected EDITIONS of our eBooks replace the old file and take over the old filename and etext number. The replaced older file is renamed. VERSIONS based on separate sources are treated as new eBooks receiving new filenames and etext numbers.

Most people start at our Web site which has the main PG search facility:

http://www.gutenberg.net

This Web site includes information about Project Gutenberg-tm, including how to make donations to the Project Gutenberg Literary Archive Foundation, how to help produce our new eBooks, and how to subscribe to our email newsletter to hear about new eBooks.

EBooks posted prior to November 2003, with eBook numbers BELOW #10000, are filed in directories based on their release date. If you want to download any of these eBooks directly, rather than using the regular search system you may utilize the following addresses and just download by the etext year.

http://www.gutenberg.net/etext06

(Or /etext 05, 04, 03, 02, 01, 00, 99, 98, 97, 96, 95, 94, 93, 92, 92, 91 or 90)

EBooks posted since November 2003, with etext numbers OVER #10000, are filed in a different way. The year of a release date is no longer part of the directory path. The path is based on the etext number (which is identical to the filename). The path to the file is made up of single digits corresponding to all but the last digit in the filename. For example an eBook of filename 10234 would be found at:

http://www.gutenberg.net/1/0/2/3/10234

or filename 24689 would be found at:
http://www.gutenberg.net/2/4/6/8/24689

An alternative method of locating eBooks:
http://www.gutenberg.net/GUTINDEX.ALL

How to Use Your Mind

A free ebook from http://manybooks.net/

9 781975 618667